HIGH PLAINS

PRESS

Riding the Edge of an Era

The Outlaw Trail

A series of trails and roads blending into an organized route that ran from Mexico to Canada.

Montana

Wyoming

Hole in
the Wall

Brown's Park

Utah

Colorado

Robbers
Roost

Arizona

New Mexico

Alma

Mexico

Riding the Edge of an Era
of an Era

Growing Up Cowboy on the Outlaw Trail

Diana Allen Kouris

HIGH PLAINS PRESS

Library of Congress Cataloging-in-Publication Data

Kouris, Diana Allen.
Riding the edge of an era :
growing up cowboy on the outlaw trail /
Diana Allen Kouris.
p. cm.
Includes index.
ISBN-13: 978-0-931271-84-7 (hard cover)
ISBN-10: 0-931271-84-3 (hard cover)
ISBN-13: 978-0-931271-85-4 (trade paper)
ISBN-10: 0-931271-85-1 (trade paper)
1. Kouris, Diana Allen. 2. Allen family.
3. Ranch life--Brown's Park--Biography. 4. Brown's Park--Biography.
I. Title.
CT275.K8375A3 2007
978'.033092--dc22
[B]   2006032661

HIGH PLAINS PRESS
403 CASSA ROAD
GLENDO, WY 82213
www.highplainspress.com
orders & catalogs: 1-800-552-7819

FIRST PRINTING

10 9 8 7 6 5 4 3 2 1

Manufactured in the United States of America

This book is dedicated to

Nonie and Bob

and

all the fine horses we rode ...

Contents

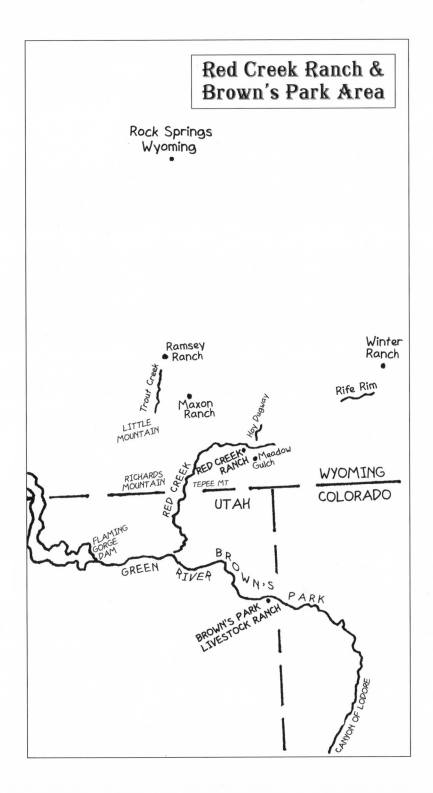

Red Creek Ranch & Brown's Park Area

Rock Springs
Wyoming
.

Ramsey
Ranch

Winter
Ranch

Trout Creek

Rife Rim

Maxon
Ranch

Hoy Dugway

LITTLE
MOUNTAIN

RED CREEK
RANCH

Meadow
Gulch

WYOMING

RICHARDS
MOUNTAIN

RED CREEK

TEPEE MT

COLORADO

UTAH

FLAMING
GORGE
DAM

BROWN'S

GREEN RIVER

PARK

BROWN'S PARK
LIVESTOCK RANCH
.

CANYON OF LODORE

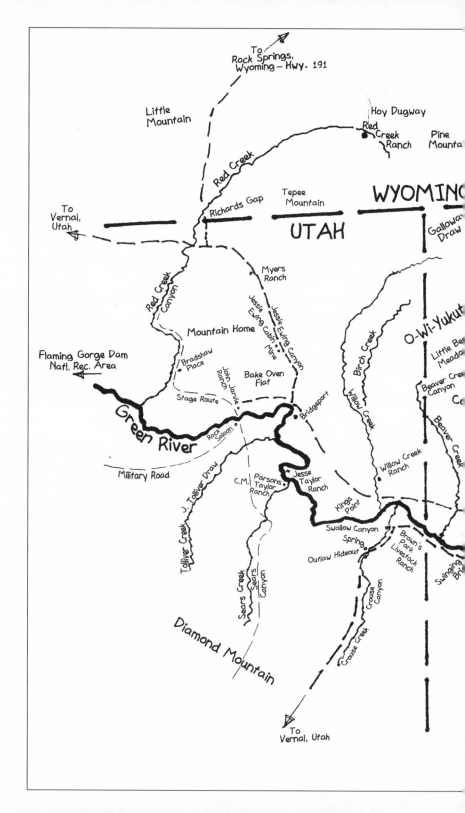

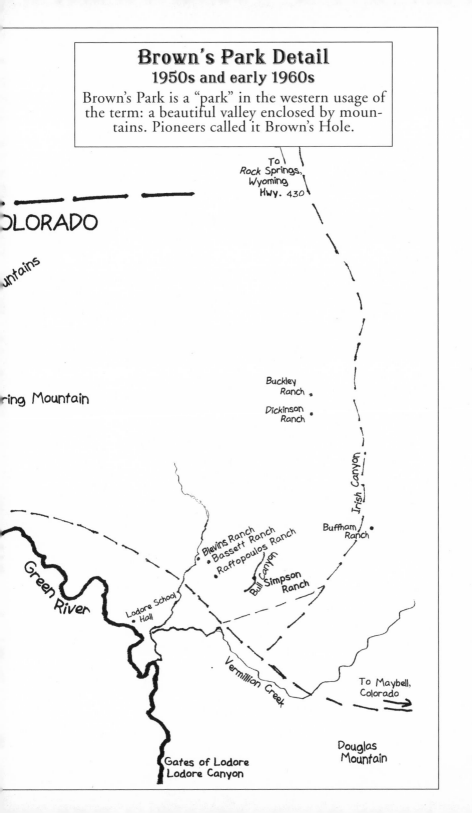

Brown's Park Detail
1950s and early 1960s

Brown's Park is a "park" in the western usage of the term: a beautiful valley enclosed by mountains. Pioneers called it Brown's Hole.

To
Rock Springs,
Wyoming
Hwy. 430

OLORADO

untains

ring Mountain

Buckley
Ranch .

Dickinson
Ranch .

Irish Canyon

Buffham
Ranch .

Blevins Ranch .
Bassett Ranch .
Raftopoulos Ranch .

Bull Canyon

Simpson
Ranch

Green River

Lodore School
. Hall

Vermillion Creek

To Maybell,
Colorado

Douglas
Mountain

Gates of Lodore
Lodore Canyon

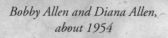
Bobby Allen and Diana Allen,
about 1954

LAUGH, DIANA! LAUGH!

We were the three youngest of the six Allen kids and we were best pals. Often given free rein to ride our cow horses on trails disappearing into sunrises and cedars, Nonie, Bobby, and I found the reflection of our heritage in enchanted places where shadows of history live. We didn't know we were riding on the far edge of an era or that our way of life was disappearing even as we lived it.

Creeks ran clear and sweet across our ranch, and the stone ledges of Diamond Mountain towered above. Our home, where outlaws once found shelter, was an 1880s log house on the Brown's Park Livestock Ranch. This ranch, also known as the Park Live, lay in the legendary "three corners" country of Utah, Colorado, and Wyoming astride the Outlaw Trail in the valley of Brown's Park. Though Brown's Park hugs the Wyoming border, the ranch spread across the valley into Colorado and Utah with its headquarters in Utah. Ever since our grandparents came here in a covered wagon in 1906, our family and hired hands raised cattle and drove them through cedar brakes and over ruby-red ledges on ancient trails and old wagon roads.

Plain for us to see, some of the trails we used were worn by centuries of thirsty animals making their way from ridges and grassy knolls to water. Others were born when tepees spread out on sandy ridges in the cedars and piñons near springs and creeks or lined the banks of the Green River in large encampments. Mountain men, who named this valley Brown's Hole, left their imprint when they came together to rendezvous and trap beaver. The ground was reshaped as pioneers carved wagon roads and trail dust lifted from the hooves of wild horses and large cattle herds. Stagecoaches and military divisions crisscrossed the area. Outlaws, including Butch Cassidy and members of the Wild Bunch, made some of their own trails as they came for sanctuary and fresh horses.

On this range we called home, old-time cowboys worked cattle on snaky broncs, and the stories and signs left behind by Native Americans and outlaws were still fresh. Without telephones or electricity, we depended on each other and read at night by the candle-like light of coal oil lamps. Tightly woven into the cowboy life, Nonie, Bobby, and I thrived within a loving family and within the bond we shared with each other and this beautiful place. Not wanting to miss any part of it, we stayed on the move.

The three of us did have a pecking order whether we were scouting the cliffs of Swallow Canyon, swiping eggs from the chicken coop to make *real* mud pies, or playing hide-and-seek on horseback along a wooded stream after dark. Occasionally Nonie knocked on Bobby, Bobby knocked on me, and then Nonie knocked on Bobby for knocking on me. Independent and contrary, Bobby didn't always agree that just because Nonie was the oldest of the three of us, she should be boss. Sometimes the two of them went at it, yanking hair and duking it out, causing Mom to holler, "You kids go outside if you're gonna act like that." When Nonie dragged Bobby out the screen door in a headlock, I hurried along behind.

Packing a rope to throw loops at fence posts, my neck, or scrambling chickens and turkeys, Robert Carl, "Bobby," was a happy, blue-eyed towhead. Nonie was a beauty. Her given name, Winona, is Native American, and her skin tanned to such a pretty shade in the summer some people believed her when she bragged, "Yup. I'm one half Apache and the other half Comanche!" Five years younger than Nonie and three younger than Bobby, I clung to their shirttails and was led to one adventure after another.

Bobby often observed life by poking it with a stick whether it was a red ant pile or the rubbery gut of a dead sheep. If something had a knob he just *had* to twist it; if it had a button he couldn't resist pushing it.

"Gimme that hammer," he ordered me. "I need to figger how this thingamajig works and see if I can fix it."

Sticking his tongue out, he bashed whatever he was working on at least a time or two. He believed just about anything could be fixed with a few good whacks from a hammer.

When Nonie was busy elsewhere, I had to hold my own. I happily followed Bobby and took my chances. I loved being with him, and as far as I was concerned he could rope the moon.

Bobby always had to keep in mind that he had to use strategy when it came to dealing with me because Mom was tuned in to hearing me bawl. Coming on the run, her apron flapping behind her, she was more awesome than any cavalry.

"C'mon in here," Bobby enticed from behind the corral poles. "Come and look at this. I've got Spot's calf good and tame for ya. He even let me put a piggin string around his middle. I'll bet he'd let ya ride him."

Before two-shakes-of-a-lamb's-tail, I was astraddle the spotted-faced milk cow calf, clutching a double strand of brown twine with both hands. Suddenly the spooked calf jerked forward and my head snapped back as he jumped into a jolting, running buck.

The corral poles shifted, worried old Spot blurred, and Bobby, throwing his hands in the air with glee, went plumb out of focus. The twine was around the steer's hide, but his hide didn't seem attached to anything and slid in all directions. Just before the corral tipped on its side, I heard Bobby yell some odd thing that sounded like *"Hook him in the shoulders!"*

The ground slugged me under the chin and my hip came down hard on top of a dry cow pie. Coming out in a whoosh, my breath sailed across the corral.

When my lungs started to function again, a full-force squall began to build. Bobby was instantly kneeling at my side. Quickly nodding his head up and down while feigning lightheartedness, he urged, "Laugh, Diana! Laugh!"

I drew a shirtsleeve across my snotty nose and started to laugh. Bobby sighed with relief. He tilted his head and looked sidelong at me and said, "Hey, you landed good—just like a gunnysack full of taters."

Walking away, I felt grainy slivers of dry manure sift and poke down the back of my neck and my hip throbbed, but I didn't care. I was just glad Bobby thought I did something well.

Bobby had good aim and he preferred a moving target. Convincing me to take off running, he'd let fly with his rope and either choke me down or hog-tie me. If he didn't have his rope handy, he lobbed rocks or sticks. Once he even hurled a four-foot metal pipe at me. He picked up the pipe from Dad's scrap pile, whirled it above his head, and persuaded me to run. I figured my best chance was to dart from side to side and outmaneuver the thing. *Thwack!* I got it square in the back of the head.

Sprawled out face first with daylight flickering, I began to wail. But Bobby was soon kneeling beside me saying, "Laugh, Diana! Laugh!"

Again he looked sidelong at me and convinced me the knot on my skull was my fault when he said, "You shouldn't've dodged. You ran right into it."

His charm continued to work when he got me to stand toe to toe and eyeball to eyeball with Muley. Muley was a large, fluffy-headed buck sheep whose greatest joy was to back up and head butt anything or anybody stupid enough to give him an opportunity. I, of course, gave him an opportunity. After he knocked me down and stomped the full length of me, I barely made a whimper before Bobby rushed to my side. He didn't have to say anything— I managed a weak giggle on my own.

Soon Bobby again had me believing my predicament was due to my mistake. Slowly shaking his head, he looked sidelong at me and said, "You should've stepped aside."

A favorite hideout was a place Nonie, Bobby, and I called the sandy spot. It was a deep wash about a half mile from the house over the top of a nearby hill. The sand there was creamy powder having been nibbled and ground for centuries by water and wind. We often had picnics there and enjoyed the soft sand, warm from the sun.

I should have known better than to go to the sandy spot alone with Bobby when he mentioned a dirt clod fight. Moisture and heat did a fine job there of forming an abundance of the firm lumps.

Before long I was positioned on one side of the wash; Bobby was on the other. The "war" was one-sided from the start. Bobby's dirt bombs and bullets sailed mightily through the air; mine fizzled out a few feet from where I launched them. The clods peppered me, stinging and exploding. I ran, dodged, slid, and hid. There was no escape.

Bobby's arm finally got tired. I was feeling pretty sorry for myself when he trotted up to me. Whining I said, "I'm not gonna come back over here with you cause you're too ornery."

He patted my shoulder, looked sidelong at me, and said, "Awww, if I didn't pick on ya, you'd think I didn't like ya."

Squinting my eyes and wrinkling my nose, I looked up and said, "Huh?"

By then he had already turned and was headed home. I brushed sand from my knees and the seat of my pants and hurried through the sagebrush, trying to catch up. Then I dug a chunk of dirt from my ear and decided he must like me an awful lot.

When we joined Nonie to search the hidden trails for our next escapade, everything was okay with me. It always turned out that way because I believed both Nonie and Bobby could twirl their lariats above their heads and give the loops wings to rope a sagebrush-scented moonrise, apricot blossoms off the wind, or anything else in between.

Top: *Bobby at 6 years old.*
Bottom: *Diana and Nonie bottle-feeding a lamb, about 1953.*

Top: *Nonie, at 8 years old.*
Bottom: *Diana, at 3 years old.*

Marie Allen, feeding bum lambs in the front yard of the ranch house, about 1954.

ON THE LOOSE

It could have been a hard way of life if not for our mother's nature to consistently reveal to us its goodness. She never complained that because of us, her brood, she traded her chaps for an apron. Nor did she say how very hard it was for her to drive off and leave Dad and her valley home each Sunday evening to take us kids—Lucille, Charlie, Les, Nonie, Bobby, and me—the hundred miles to Rock Springs, Wyoming, and remain there during the week to take care of us while we went to school.

Although there was a school on the far edge of the Colorado side of Brown's Park, it served students only through the eighth grade. Our ages spanned thirteen years. Mom and Dad conducted their financial business, did most of their shopping, and received medical care in Rock Springs, just as many Brown's Park families had since the 1800s. Years earlier, Mom and Dad had purchased a home in Rock Springs so Mom could be near her parents to help care for her father when he became gravely ill. Mom and Dad could have sent us to boarding school. I heard them speak of it only once. Instead, so we wouldn't have to, Mom and Dad made the sacrifices.

During the school months, we could hardly wait until Friday each week when we always crowded into the car and headed from Rock Springs to the ranch where Dad waited. Sunday evenings, when we left to go back to town, came much too quickly. But when the end of the school year arrived in May, we were free to go to the ranch and stay there until fall.

In the spring of 1955 I was five years old. School had finally finished for the year when Mom called out, "Come on, you kids, you'd better pile in or you're liable to get left!" Hopping with excitement, I hurried to the car, remembering we had left Bobby behind once. We didn't miss him until someone noticed we had an extra bottle of pop.

Lucille had graduated a year earlier and was now living in Denver, attending business college. Our older brothers, Charles Edward, "Charlie," and William Leslie, "Les," were seventeen and thirteen, respectively, and had dibs on the front seat. Nonie, Bobby, and I shared the back with Midget, our little white dog. We didn't care where we rode as long as we were headed to the ranch.

Two and a half hours later and about a half mile from our ranch house, Nonie, Bobby, and I couldn't sit still. Stepping on the brake, Mom said, "You little snerts better run some of it off or you'll never be able to sleep tonight. We'll see you at the house when you get there." The car stopped and the three of us flung the doors open and jumped into the moonlight drenched with spring.

A foothill to Diamond Mountain we called the rocky hill banked our left. Just off the slope on our other side glistened two shallow lakes surrounded by marshes with thick patches of reeds, hollow-stemmed rushes, and furry cattails. Dwelling there were families of ducks, geese, rails, herons, swans, and cranes. Huge numbers of toads and frogs gossiped and tried to out-yell each other. All the night songs blended to sound like a grand concert hall filled with an orchestra tuning its instruments.

As we ran for home, our legs uncoiled like snow-bent saplings finally released. We passed through pockets of air with one feeling cool and the next warm. The air smelled lush and fruity like melon, and as it filled our lungs, no words, only giggles, spilled out. Nearing the house, we crossed the bridge over Crouse Creek. The water jumped and bucked beneath us, rushing to green pastures.

After dashing up a small hill, we passed the shop and granary. Finally we skipped through an archway of deer antlers and honeysuckle blooms as we entered the yard. A soft light coming from the kitchen window showed off three red geraniums on the sill as Ring, Dad's border collie, hurried to greet us. The white cat gave us a second of her time, and several peacocks roosting in the trees used our racket for an excuse to start hollering. Their calls were a sure sound of spring, and home.

Out of breath we trampled through the screen door and across the screened porch that served as Mom and Dad's summer bedroom. After hurrying into the kitchen, we stopped at a small table holding two buckets filled with creek water fresh from Diamond Mountain's sun-toasted snowbanks. The cool water was so luscious that the more we drank, the thirstier we became. We drained one dipperful after another until we actually sloshed a little when we walked.

Sliding onto the bench behind the long kitchen table, we were more than ready to eat the supper Dad had prepared. We lapped up steaming bowls of rice mixed with milk and sugar and bit into thick slices of mom's crusty bread spread with hand-churned butter.

Later when the boys sauntered to the bunkhouse, Nonie and I were happy to tag along behind Mom down the pathway to the outhouse. We always loved these times when we had her all to ourselves. It was a tender place, where the stars hung in sterling clusters no farther away than a whisper could be heard. It was always a time for talking, and listening.

Feeling a bit uneasy I said, "Momma, I heard you visiting with your friend yesterday. I heard her say that the doctor told you that you weren't to dare have any more kids after Nonie. So how come you had me and Bobby?"

Without the slightest hesitation, Mom cupped my face in the softness of her hands, looked into my eyes, and said, "Oh, sweetheart, because no matter what, with all my heart, I wanted one more little boy and one more little girl."

Many years later I would learn that the forbidden pregnancies were not planned. Rather, Mom had cried for days with the news and was both frightened and ill. But because she chose to answer my question as she did, after Nonie blew out the flame of the coal oil lamp and we snuggled into our bed, I had a strong sense of self-worth. I drew my fists up under my chin and smiled, holding tightly to the warmth that Mom had forever lit inside me.

Daybreak hadn't yet arrived when Nonie bounced upright in bed. "C'mon," she whispered. "Be quiet, though. If Mom hears us she'll make us stay in bed."

After dressing in a hurry, we headed for the door. On tiptoe, we walked bull-legged to keep our Levis, ironed stiff by the cold linoleum floor, from giving us away with any raspy sounds. We spotted Bobby standing beneath a spreading apricot tree impatiently waving for us to hurry.

Soon we were out of the yard gate trying to outrun each other. We'd made good our escape, and the morning, the ranch, and summer swirled around us offering so much we could barely stand it.

Just to the northwest the Green River flowed beneath King's Point as it came through the red mouth of Swallow Canyon. Explorer John Wesley Powell named the canyon in 1869 for the flocks of swallows that nested among its high cliffs. Flooding its banks each spring, the river watered the willows, cottonwoods, and thick grasses of the low-lying bottoms that edged the ranch.

Our house was surrounded by pastures and hay meadows that Dad kept irrigated with the creeks flowing from Diamond Mountain. Along the creeks, mature plum and crab apple trees blossomed and bore fruit in the midst of thickets of shade trees and shrubs.

Mom always encouraged our sister Lucille's love for tending flowers, and this year her bearded irises stood extra tall and in bloom. Poppies, columbines, and hollyhocks were well on their way. There were three apricot trees within the fenced yard along with lilacs, honeysuckle, and a large patch of wild roses loaded with pink buds. Tall boxelder, cottonwood, aspen, and elm trees watched over it all.

The log house, put together with wooden pegs instead of nails, was old and comfortable, gaining its personality from outlaws, cowboys, ranch women, and kids who called it home throughout the decades. It had a dirt roof, plaster walls, and tongue-and-groove ceilings. Cool in the summer, it stayed cozy in the winter by capturing the heat from the cookstove and a heater in the center of the living room that burned both wood and coal. As a youngster Robert LeRoy Parker (Butch Cassidy) lived here when he worked for Charlie Crouse, founder of the ranch. Later, after Cassidy became an outlaw, he and other outlaws came here for safe haven, food, and fresh thoroughbred horses.

Our own horses fed this morning in the same pastures where, not so very long ago, the outlaws' horses fed. Looking up, the geldings watched us through the bluish darkness as if they couldn't believe we three whelps were already on the loose.

"OK," Nonie said. "Whatever you do, don't let'em see the bridles."

Dragging our bridles behind us, we made our approach across the pasture cautiously, rattling some dried corn in a coffee can. We were lucky they couldn't resist.

Nonie caught Dollycolt, a pretty bay gelding whose mother had been named Dolly. Ever since Dad loaned him to a group of Boy Scouts, he reared now and then. But Nonie didn't mind a little thing like that.

Bobby got the bit in Smokey's mouth. White with reddish freckles, Smokey was racehorse tall. He must have relished the shoots of grass surrounding burdock because he always had a big wad of burs pin-curling his forelock. Bobby gripped Smokey's mane and swung onto his back. Smokey held his head high and his breath whistled in and out of his lungs. Before he came into our family, Smokey was winded by someone who ran him to exhaustion. Still, he was always poised for that next race.

My horse, Bollie, was a blood bay with a blaze face and short tail. He had the body and gentleness of a workhorse but lacked the energy. I packed a little willow switch to give him some incentive. Nonie grunted as she gave me a boost, and I perched on Bollie's soft back with my legs extending nearly straight out as we headed for the saddle shed.

Dawn was still stingy with the light as we saddled up and made our way past the house and then toward Swallow Canyon. We came to a stop on a hillside at the gravesite of brothers Charlie and Albert Seger. We knew Charlie was killed with a knife during a poker game in the kitchen of our log house back in 1891.

Our imaginations transformed us into cowboy heroes. Turning our horses toward the cedars, we rode three abreast, acting cocky and talking tough.

I hurled spit through the gap between my front teeth and imagined it to be tobacco juice and said, "Hey, boys, do ya think we otta chase down them outlaws today?"

"Yeah," Bobby answered. "I know where their hideout is."

Nonie kicked Dollycolt into a trot. "Well, we'd better hurry. If they get wind we're comin', they'll hightail it."

As we trotted through the sagebrush and into the cedars, Smokey strained against Bobby's grip on the reins, and Bollie switched his tail with every willow swat. With the outlaws cornered and in jail within minutes, we rode on, following a deer trail. When we came into a clearing, we were suddenly cast into an ancient world of majestic cliffs and boulders.

"It's a tumbledown castle," Bobby whispered.

We slipped from our horses and ran along the sandstone walls. The red rock was embroidered with moss and other tiny plants creating tapestries revealing knights and kings and toppled palace walls. We agreed that the location of Tumbledown Castle would forever be our secret.

Bobby climbed back in the saddle and said, "I'm ready for a stack of hotcakes."

"Yeah," Nonie agreed, "with a bunch of chokecherry syrup."

I yelled from behind. "I'm gonna have two eggs this mornin'. Maybe even three!"

Nonie and Bobby rode a ways in front of me, moving out of the cedars and into the creamy blue rising with the sun. We heard Mom's voice calling us to breakfast so we nudged our horses into a trot.

Watching Nonie and Bobby ride into the morning, I couldn't know of all the sunrises and sunsets we were destined to share. I did know, as I patted Bollie on the neck and jogged along in the rear, that I was luckiest and happiest whenever they were near.

Right top: *The Brown's Park Livestock Ranch house in the 1880s. Ranch founders, Charlie and Mary Crouse, stand near the doorway.*
Right: *Rock Springs, Wyoming, in 1951. Back row: Melvin Garrison (cousin), Lucille, Charlie, and Diana. Front row: Les holding Midget, Bobby holding a neighborhood cat, and Nonie.*

Marie Taylor and Bill Allen when they were courting, in 1931.

TOGETHER THEY DANCED

Nonie and I awoke at dawn to the morning harmony that was our mom and dad. Their voices and the rhythmic *ploop-ploop* of Dad beating the sour milk hotcake batter came to us on the aroma of coffee and bacon. Burrowed in the warmth of the blankets, we clung to those few minutes before we were called to get up.

Our dad and mom, Bill and Marie, always made the ranch breakfasts together, cooking on a wood-burning cookstove until the recent purchase of a restaurant style range that came with a large griddle, six burners, and two ovens. Using the fermenting milk from a crockery jar kept on the counter as a main ingredient, Dad stirred his batter in a particular stainless steel bowl while Mom prepared the rest of the meal.

He sometimes called her Marie; she occasionally called him Bill or "Pappy Turner." Most of the time they simply called each other Mom and Dad. Though they had matching dark hair and blue eyes and both were energetic and forthright, they were very different people in the way they viewed life.

Born in 1915, Mom told us her pioneer-like childhood in Brown's Park was magical. She adored her father, C.M. Taylor, who taught her to ride and rope and to find the joy and beauty in a blizzard as well as in the song of a meadowlark. She, in turn, showed us that no matter how tough a job became, there was always an opportunity to step back and look for a reason to grin.

Dad, two years older than Mom, was just three years old when his father died. On his own from a very early age, Dad viewed work solely as a serious matter of survival. But together Mom and Dad were cattle ranchers and they were partners. The six of us kids were all expected to follow their directions, work hard, and do our parts.

Summer meant a stream of vacationing friends and relatives. The kitchen table, easily seating ten people, was sometimes reset in shifts to get everyone fed. Some nights, pillows were placed at each end of a couple of beds and kids settled down in rows. People and laughter filled up all the spaces as Mom, somehow, made room for everyone.

Sweat trickled down Mom's face as she cooked and cleaned. She scrubbed mounds of washing on a washboard by using water packed from the creek and heated in teakettles, and she dried bedding, towels, hankies, denim jeans, shirts, and underwear on the line in the sunshine. After gathering the laundry off the line, Mom sprinkled water over the items that needed to be ironed and then rolled and stacked them in bushel baskets. With heavy irons heated on the stove, she pressed and creased each piece.

We tended a huge garden. In the fall the cellar was filled with potatoes, onions, carrots, beets, turnips, winter squash, and apples. We all went together with a picnic lunch to pick clusters of wild chokecherries and elderberries to process into syrups and jellies. Windows steamed and the kitchen became a cannery as Mom filled jar after shiny jar with pickles, vegetables, fruits, and fruity spreads and syrups.

Mom baked bread, cookies, jellyrolls, cream puffs, cakes, and pies galore and took pride in serving platters stacked high with satisfying food. She gladly taught us the methods and histories of each recipe. Holidays were celebrated with decorations and special meals, and Mom made sure each of our birthdays, always, was highlighted with a decorated cake.

Squatting on a wobbly, one-legged milk stool, Mom often took off her gold-colored Stetson and leaned her forehead into the warm flank of the milk cow. Squeezing the teats, she closed her eyes and dreamed her dreams to the rhythm of the milk streaming into the metal bucket. After Mom strained the milk through cheesecloth, she chilled some milk for drinking, left some to clabber to make into cottage cheese, and separated the rest and churned it into butter.

Though it hurt her to do so, she was not squeamish when it was necessary to grab up a chubby hen and prepare her for the skillet or a turkey for the oven. Such necessary jobs she accomplished with skill and swiftness.

Mom sometimes helped in the hayfield, running the baler in the fragrant heat, but remained in her height of happiness when she got the opportunity to ride after cattle. Trailing behind the herd of red and white Herefords, she twirled her rope at her side while occasionally letting the knotted end graze the tail of a cow to urge her to hurry. "Come on, ole girls, step along," she'd say. Even though she couldn't carry much of a tune, nothing was more endearing than the sound of her voice serenading the herd and us with the words to the cowboy ballads "Little Joe the Wrangler" and "Billy Vanero."

⁂

Nonie and I turned over in our bed and got a whiff of sauerkraut sizzling in a skillet, which promised that breakfast would be a family favorite. Our first hotcake, accompanied by bacon, would be layered with butter, a fried egg, homemade sauerkraut, and then topped with ketchup. Mom would likely say, "This'll stick to your ribs and fill up your hollow legs. It's going to be a long, tough day in the saddle."

I thought about the day before when we had gathered and sorted cattle, getting ready to take the main herd to the summer range in Colorado on Cold Spring Mountain. We had all been on edge because Dad had one way of working cows, especially in the corral, and that was the scary way! He was stern with his orders and expectations. We stayed so poised for action that a friend once said we looked as though our eyeballs could be knocked off with a stick and a tune played on our necks. If told to turn a cow, we knew we'd better do so. Dad didn't have to raise a hand to us because his mere glance of disapproval was thunderous.

Dad was often distant. During meals his worries and responsibilities sometimes overtook him, and with a frown he completely removed himself from our conversation and laughter. But he was not mean. And he was our Easter bunny. Each year he got up very early and hurried outside to hide treats and the dozens of eggs we'd colored the night before. He giggled and his eyes lit up with enjoyment as we dashed in all directions, squealing with the treasures that were filling our baskets.

Put a bat in Dad's hands and he became a kid again. Whenever we formed our teams in the pasture below the house for a game of baseball, Dad stopped whatever he was doing to play with us. Always able to knock the ball flying, he dashed for the bases, laughing until tears ran down his face. And there were countless times when he joined us to play kick-the-can and Annie-Annie-over.

Dad took great pleasure in turning water down the ditches and watching it spread across the pastures and fields, giving them life. He got so excited during rainstorms that he hurried from window to window to watch it pour down and spatter the earth. If one of us kids made the mistake of getting in his way in front of a window, he'd nearly run us over and never even notice.

Each fall Mom and Dad hosted a small number of deer hunters who came from across the United States. Mom did the cooking and Dad guided the fun-loving men on successful hunting trips. The best times were had at the end of the day when they sat down to devour Mom's supper while telling one comical story after the other.

The Lodore School Hall has been an important part of the social life in Brown's Park since 1911 when it was built. Located on the Colorado side of the valley on a sagebrush and greasewood covered ridge, it sits near the river and has a beautiful view of majestic Lodore Canyon. Although when Mom was a young girl she had to board with other families to go to school there because of the distance from home, Mom loved it. The building welcomed many school children through the years, off and on, until 1947; after that, the Lodore School Hall continued to be used for all kinds of functions. Its dances drew large crowds from near and far. The plaster walls, oak floor, and surrounding sagebrush and greasewood got soaked clear through with the music from fiddles and guitars. Although it was quietly aging, the Lodore School Hall always came wide awake when the first notes lit up the air, and it usually stayed awake until dawn.

During dances at the Lodore School, where families came together to have fun, Dad called the square dances without a microphone, served as the bouncer making sure no liquor was ever brought inside, and danced the two-step with Mom in flawless rhythm. When he chose to play, he played hard and gave it his all. The same was true of his work.

The ranch was serious business to Dad. And the cattle herd was the ranch. The cycle of the seasons dictated the work surrounding calving, branding, fencing, doctoring, trailing, irrigating, haying, gathering, shipping, and feeding. Almost everything Dad did revolved around the well-being of the herd.

Mom and Dad made it through a lot together. They married when Dad was just nineteen and Mom was two years younger. Through the years their land holdings, cattle herd, and family grew as they developed their business called Allen Livestock. They were deeply saddened when on March 30, 1943, a baby daughter they named Barbara Lee died at birth. By 1946 they had five young children.

The weight of life was heavy for Mom and Dad. A distance grew between them and their marriage wavered under the strain. Then they faced an event that both shattered and mended them.

Mom often talked to us about Billie Dee, her third-born and Dad's namesake. Speaking of her daughter's almond-shaped eyes and the sunshine in her singing voice, Mom always concluded by softly saying, "Don't mention Billie Dee in front of Dad—it just hurts him too much."

⤶

The morning of the fourth day in June in 1946 held glorious expectations. A picnic on Cold Spring Mountain among the wildflowers, aspens, and pines to celebrate Lucille's tenth birthday was the destination. Dad's blue stock truck was loaded with a passel of kids and plenty of food, including Lucille's favorite banana cake.

Pregnant with Bobby, Mom held Nonie on her lap in the seat beside Dad as he steered the truck along a rutted road. Surrounded by a secure stock rack, the Allen children and neighbor children from the Willow Creek Ranch—Georgann, Marylou, and Zander Radosevich—laughed in the back of the stock truck as it moved through the sweet mountain air.

No one noticed when seven-year-old Billie Dee climbed on top of a fifty-gallon barrel that stood in a corner next to the cab. No one saw that her perch was flush with the top of the rack. No one paid very much attention when the truck slowed, then dropped into a rut, causing the truck to jerk sideways. But the children saw the unexpected motion yank Billie Dee from her seat and fling her over the top of the rack. They screamed as she flew headfirst, striking a cedar fence post and then a dirt bank, which roughly threw her away and into the path of the rear dual wheels of her father's truck.

The screams caused Dad to slam on the brake. Mom threw Nonie from her lap, desperate to get out the door. Reaching Billy Dee first, Dad saw the tire marks across his little girl's face and chest and the blood gush from her mouth when he tried to lift her.

Mom kneeled over Billie Dee and felt herself begin to drift and break. Then she looked up and saw the faces of the terrified children peering from the truck. The sight poured into her, telling her she had to resist the darkness.

Dad splintered. Grabbing his hat off his head, he cried out as he furiously threw it to the ground and stomped it. Again and again, his wails of agony echoed through the trees and across the ridges.

Mom carried Billy Dee into the shade beneath a grove of willows. Understanding their need to do something, anything, Mom spoke gently to the children. "Hurry, now. Fill your hats with water from the creek and bring it to me."

The youngsters ran swiftly, back and forth, with their hats dripping. While Mom held Nonie against her shoulder with one hand, she used her other to wash Billie Dee's face with soft pats and caresses that said the loving and sorrowful words to her child that she could not speak.

Eventually Dad's screams silenced and everyone quietly returned to the truck. Mom drove the short distance back to Wright and Margaret Dickinson's ranch house (later known as the Buckley place). While Margaret took the three Radosevich kids back to their home in Brown's Park, Wright drove the dazed Allen family to Rock Springs. Instead of giving in to the hysteria Mom longed to release, she sat in the back of the truck as it sped toward town and held herself steady, while she cradled Billie Dee's body close to her own.

During the days that followed, Dad remained devastated. Mom knew that. The house was filled with people when she watched him from across the room. She saw the anguish in his face as she walked toward him carrying Nonie. Stopping in front of him, she looked into his eyes, then gently placed their youngest child in his arms.

Dad's body went limp as he leaned into his wife. In that instant, the love they shared became their warmth and strength. The differences between them fell away because they held no more significance. The tattered bond between them was mending and together they would heal.

Later that evening, after everyone left, Mom walked into a bedroom and closed the door. It was then that her private time came. She finally gave in to the grieving torment, and it turned loose and engulfed her....

⁂

Still lingering in bed that June morning nine years later, Nonie and I heard Mom's happy voice call, "Hop up, girls. Hop like a bunny. Time's-a-wastin'. Dad just went out to the bunkhouse to call the boys. If you hurry, you can get dressed in the kitchen where it's warm."

We threw the covers back, jumped from our bed, and scooped up our clothes on the run. We went with the certainty that there was always plenty of good food, warm beds, affection, discipline, hard work, and play to go around. Our parents were cattle ranchers. They were partners. And together, they danced.

Left top: *Bill Allen, in 1931.*
Left below: *A glimpse at Brown's Park.*
Top: *The Lodore School just after it was built in 1911.*
Above: *Lucille, Billie Dee, Marie, Charlie, and Bill Allen, about 1940.*

Les and Comet when they were both youngsters.

PILLYCHICH
AND THE BUCKSKIN COMET

We watched a cocky, white rooster scratch and peck the ground, making his way under the belly of a buckskin gelding grazing on the lawn. They were not friends. Mostly they were indifferent to each other. But they were alike in that both had been pampered and spoiled by us Allen kids.

A couple years earlier, having run out of patience waiting for her last egg to hatch, a plump white hen gathered her obedient chicks and left the nest. We found the abandoned egg, and Lucille cuddled and kept it warm throughout the night. First thing the next morning, the chick announced his arrival with loud chirps. Hand fed with cornmeal dampened with water, the baby thrived.

Family friends arrived at the ranch one afternoon, and the chick immediately became the center of attention. The daughter, who had a speech impediment, took off running to catch the young chicken. Round and round the car they went. The girl meant to say, *Come here you dumb little pretty chick.* Instead she squealed, "Come here you dom lill pilly chich." Everyone laughed, including the girl, and the chick was named Pillychich.

Pillychich grew into a huge, white, very bossy rooster, claiming not only the barnyard as his to rule but the dooryard as well. He crowed, strutted, and bullied almost anything that caught his eye. Grandma Christensen tended to catch his eye.

Grandma and Grandpa Christensen, Dad's mother and stepfather, spent a good part of each summer with us. Grandpa Christensen was a kind, petite fellow who always wore striped bib overalls.

He loved his family and life on the ranch. He mowed hay for Dad and milked cows for Mom, yet he always saved time for his grand-kids.

Grandpa showed us he could munch an apple with nary a tooth, and because he had no teeth, he could touch his nose with his chin. He taught us how to *really* enjoy chunks of homemade bread covered with milk in a bowl and seasoned with salt and pep-per—preferably accompanied by a couple of green onions and crispy radishes.

Always wearing dresses covered with cotton aprons, Grandma Christensen tucked her white hair beneath a net and rolled her nylons to a halt at the knee. Usually content to stay in low gear, she spent most of every day sitting in a corner of the kitchen crocheting pretty doilies.

After finishing supper one evening, Grandma drew a white sweater across her shoulders and very slowly stepped out the porch screen door and onto the rock walkway. Dishes clanked behind her in the kitchen and teakettles whistled that the water they held was ready for the dishpan.

Suddenly screeches erupted outside, causing us all to jump. Big-eyed we looked at each other and in unison said, "Grandma!"

We ran outside and found her, fit-to-be-tied. After some commotion and a little dress straightening, the adults smoothed Grandma's "ruffled feathers," and Pillychich showed off the feathers in his pearly jacket as he sashayed toward the coop where his pole roost waited.

Grandma had bypassed the journey down the path to the out-house, deciding to hike her skirts behind a tree. In the middle of her business, she was roughly rear-ended, ridden, and spurred by our white ruffian.

As we hid our giggles, Mom said, "I guess I'm gonna have to mash Pillychich's toe again to give him something else to think about."

That was an early day solution to keep a barnyard bully from getting completely out of hand. The creature with the sore toe was kept busy nursing the injury, which sometimes prevented serious injury to those unfortunate enough to be on the lower end of the chain of command.

The buckskin horse named Comet wasn't really a bully and he didn't need his toe mashed, but he sure could be cantankerous and balky. Comet was an irresistible colt and, with an abundance of affection and attention, he became a sly gelding. Most of the time he was very tame and not interested in hurrying. Early on he figured out how to open gates and how to give the "soft eye" to get a sugar cube or a peanut butter and honey sandwich.

Mom shook her head and said, "He's just too cussed smart for his own good."

One evening we were riding a few miles downriver from home when the sun lowered behind the mountains of Swallow Canyon. I was happy to be riding Comet, but we had been in the saddle since morning. Tired and hungry, we were glad to be able to start trotting our horses toward the blush of color where Mom would have supper waiting.

Without warning, the smart aleck I was riding humped his buckskin back and jumped, flipping me end-over-end into the sagebrush. Before my sight completely cleared, Dad propped me back in my saddle and stuck the reins in my hands.

"Now, you'd better hang on," he mumbled.

Tears stung my eyes as I nodded that I would. But Comet was eyeballing me over the top of his black mane. He'd just discovered how simple it was to pitch this little five-year-old nuisance head-first.

Traveling no more than a few yards, Comet suddenly kicked up his heels, sending me airborne. Looking back over their shoulders, everyone stopped and then lowered their heads with impatience. Stern-faced, Dad picked me up and again placed me square in the saddle.

"I thought I told you to hang on."

A few minutes later when I plowed the ground for the third time, I felt gray branches snap as dust and sagebrush leaves puffed into a cloud. Dazed, I lifted my head and saw everyone looking down at me from their horses. There was still a long way to go, and this constant delay was obviously aggravating.

Now wait a minute, you guys, I wanted to yell. *I'm the one hitting the ground every five minutes and then getting drug up by the seat of my britches and stuck back on this wild-eyed bronc.* But I knew Comet's crow-hopping didn't carry much weight with these cowhands, so I'd better keep still. They only knew that I wasn't staying on my horse, and that was making for a long ride home.

After once again placing me on the hard leather seat, Dad grabbed hold of my bridle reins and climbed on his horse. Dad pulled Comet alongside and said to the horse, "Now, you'd better tend to your business."

Comet was instantly subdued. By then he was probably tired of messing around. Picking up his head, he broke into a trot beside Dad's horse, ready to go home.

I gripped the saddle horn with both hands and hung on for all I was worth as I bobbed along in tearful silence. I knew Comet had gotten the best of me, but that was nothing new.

A few days later, Nonie peeked around the corner of the house and saw Comet with his head down feeding on the lawn. Although he wasn't saddled, he was bridled and dragging the leather reins along as he went.

Comet had the whole game figured out and almost always played it his way: if we led him close to something we could climb on so we could jump on his back, he usually stood still until the second before we jumped, then he stepped just out of reach. Sometimes we'd go round and round for an hour or two before he'd decide to be ridden.

Nonie whispered to Bobby and me, "I'm gonna get on Comet's neck while his head's down."

Nonchalantly she picked up the reins as Comet continued to eat. Suddenly she threw one leg over his neck and grabbed his mane with both hands. Comet lifted his head and Nonie slid into place on his back.

"Hey, it worked!" she yelled.

It worked so well that a few minutes later she decided to give it another try. Throwing her leg over Comet's neck, she was caught by surprise when he jerked his head skyward, hurling her halfway across the yard. We didn't give it up, though, and tried to mount that way several more times. Occasionally he gave us our way; usually he pitched us over his rump.

Sometimes Comet let us ride him without a saddle or bridle, handling fine with just a piece of baling twine around his neck. We often brought the milk cows, Spot and Blackie, into the corral from the pasture that way.

One evening Mom was on her way to get the milk cows and their calves when she spotted Comet. When she later got back to the house, the woman who'd grown up a top hand cowgirl bent over with laughter.

"Well, there's no fool like an old fool," she said. "I figured I'd just ride Comet like you kids do to get the cows. But I no more than jumped up on him when he made up his mind to back into that tangle of plum trees along the creek. I gave it to him with everything I had, but that stinker just kept going backward until he brushed me off, right over his head."

Wiping tears from her cheeks, she continued. "I sprawled out there on all fours and that character just stood there and watched me. I gave it up and *walked* after the cows."

During the heat of the day one afternoon, I hugged on Comet and braided his mane. We were taking it easy in the shade of the trees behind the house. A couple of times Comet exhaled in long, bored sighs, having had about all of my company he could stand. But I was in the mood for a ride.

I climbed the side of a tree and jumped on his bare back. When I nudged his sides with my heels, he didn't move. I tried it again but immediately tensed when, instead of moving forward, he started bobbing his head and backing up. Feeling the leafy branches scrape my back and the top of my head, I bent over and yelled, "Comet!"

I hunkered down and tried to grip with my legs, but there was never any hope. Sliding off the side of Comet's neck, I landed in a heap beneath an apricot tree.

Comet then lifted a front hoof and stepped down on my left forearm. I squealed in terror. But Comet ignored my bawling and only put pressure on my arm when I tried to pull free. He never stepped hard enough to hurt me, only hard enough to hold me still as he lowered his head and began to eat.

My yelling finally brought Nonie and Bobby skidding around the corner. From where I lay, Comet looked like a gigantic, buckskin beast. From where they stood, the sight was at first surprising, then hilarious. But they stopped their hee-hawing when Mom barreled around the corner and scooped me up to make sure all my parts were attached.

By supper my trauma became a comedy to share with Dad and the others. Each one of us had to take a turn telling it our way. We laughed so hard in the trying that it took half the meal to get it told.

It wasn't long after when Comet proved, as Mom had said long ago, that he was too smart for his own good. He not only worked the wire loop off the pasture gate but also gnawed loose the leather strap holding a door closed in the tack shed. Inside was a fifty-gallon barrel filled with grain. The grain in small amounts was the greatest of treats for a horse. But, of course, Comet only knew that he had a barrel full of the rich-smelling stuff right under his nose.

When we found him, Comet was deathly ill. The overdose poisoned his system and sent his body temperature soaring. His groans broke our hearts and we all cried. With obvious, severe pain in his feet, he stood still, sweating and reluctant to move.

"Well, he's foundered," Dad said. "There's not much we can do but try soaking his feet in cold water to give him some relief and just give him time to fight his way through this."

Comet partially recovered. The front of his smooth hooves turned ugly and corrugated, and he especially favored his right front foot, making him slightly lame. But the handsome gelding remained part of the family and did some important work through the years of his long life. We eventually gave him a couple of important new duties. Since he was pretty much cured of his antics, Comet became both a prospector's companion and a trusted babysitter.

Murty "Murt" Taylor, one of the joys of our childhood, was a gaunt, toothless, coarse old codger from Riverton, Wyoming. Born in 1888, he swore that when he was younger he and a companion discovered a gold mine nearby, at the foot of Diamond Mountain.

Rubbing the top of his head, which he kept shaved with a battery-powered razor, he'd say, "I know that gold's up there so you daresn't tell anyone what I'm looking for or they'll beat me to it.

When I got sick and couldn't do much for several years, I lost track of just where it exactly is."

Explaining about his illness he continued, "The doctors took half my stomach out before it was all said and done. To this day I can't digest my food worth a darn. They claimed I died on the operating table for about three minutes and they figured I should have seen Heaven or something, but I didn't see anything at all. I just know I was bad sick, and when I finally got back on my feet, I couldn't remember some things. So now I'm just tryin' to get it all figured out."

For many summers Murt kept the gold mine as the main purpose in his life as he and his little dog made their way to Brown's Park from Riverton, dragging a homemade camper behind a Jeep. Sharing occasional meals with us, he almost always suffered severe nausea afterward. Turning pale, he usually drank a glass of water mixed with baking soda. He then sat down, held his head, and belched repeatedly. Within an hour or so his suffering passed and he went on with his day.

Murt helped out around the place, occasionally sleeping a night or two in the bunkhouse. But he spent most of his time camped at the foot of the mountain then walking, or sometimes riding Comet, along its ridges.

Nonie, Bobby, and I were especially close to this man who had great wisdom about many subjects. We were always fascinated with Murt and the way he stuck a cigarette half its length into his mouth and wallowed it around before lighting it up with a lighter's flame the size of a blowtorch. We listened closely as he told us of his life in the early days. We wanted to believe the mine was real and sometimes helped him search. Down deep we figured Mom and Dad were right, and it was just something he dreamed up during his illness.

Comet seemed content with the slow pace of his days spent with Murt. Murt and Comet made quite a pair. "He takes his time stepping through the cedars with me," Murt said. "That's just the way we both like it. The old bugger looks me square in the eye. I've gotta say he's awful good company."

Murt returned each spring for several more years, spending more and more time with us and less time searching for his lost mine. When his health failed and he could no longer leave the rooming house where he lived in Riverton to make the journey to the ranch, we put handwritten notes in the packages of freshly baked goods Mom often sent him.

To the end of his life we showed Murt he shared in the bond of a loving family. Although he never found the gold, perhaps, through us, he did find the treasure he desired most after all.

Besides being Murt's companion, Comet would have another important job: when Lucille married and the first grandchild in our family arrived, Comet became a babysitter. Through the years, it would be up to the wise gelding to be extra gentle as he delighted the little ones and gave them their first horseback rides.

Pillychich, too, lived a long life. When the younger, stronger roosters bumped him from his place on the highest rung, he went quietly about his days. He eventually died of old age and toppled off the roost in his sleep.

⚭

Comet and Pillychich were as much a part of what gave life to the Brown's Park Livestock Ranch as warm, soaking rains. The two critters were a little bit ornery and more than a tad spoiled, but they belonged there—just like Nonie, Bobby, and me.

Left: *Murt Taylor at the ranch.*
Below: *Charlie and Comet in the spring of 1951.*

Top: *Diana and Bobby and their favorite cow for riding: Blackie, the milk cow.*
Above: *Allen Livestock cattle in the corrals in the mid-1950s.*

Top: *A ranch playground for the Allen kids.*

Left: *Lucille bottle-feeding a lamb.*

Members of the Allen Livestock wild herd.

A BUTTERMILK MOON

The sun stretched its time in the sky, creating long summer days, and our family used every hour because of the work that needed to be done from breaking horses to putting up hay. Helping Mom around the house, Nonie, Bobby, and I pulled weeds in the garden, churned butter until our arms ached, carried fruit and vegetable scraps to the pigs, cracked walnuts, hung out the wash, gathered eggs, watched out for burdock and chopped it down before it could spread its burs, and did a slew of other chores.

Sometimes these jobs were just plain work, and a little laziness turned into complaining now and then. But Mom did not tolerate whining. Instead, she encouraged our natural inclination to have fun. So most of the time we made games out of the chores we had to do. And because of Mom's eagerness to compliment us for jobs well done, we strived to do them well. From that, we gained daily doses of the feeling that we counted and our help was an important part of what made the ranch run.

Although there was a lot of work to do, Mom made sure we had plenty of time for ourselves. She often helped us make picnic lunches because she understood our need to run free. In the coming years the most strenuous summer work would pass to us. But for now, it was Dad, Grandpa, the older kids, and hired men who were in the hayfield working up a sweat.

Leaning forward in the saddle, Nonie yanked a green apple loose from an elderly tree growing in the orchard at the top of the huge alfalfa field. When she munched on a juicy chunk, her nose holes flared from the tartness. "Mmmmm," she puckered. "Mom says these'll give us the bellyache, but I don't get bellyaches." The summer heat baking the air around the fruit trees smelled like warm dessert. Breathing it in, Nonie, Bobby, and I picked all the apples we could carry. Sprinkled with salt, green apples were one of the many pleasures of haying season.

Located at the foot of Diamond Mountain on the bench of a hill not far from the house, the orchard was planted in the 1880s by ranch owner Charlie Crouse. It's likely outlaws Butch Cassidy, Matt Warner, Elzy Lay, and others pulled an apple or two from young branches because in those days a secluded cabin Charlie Crouse let them use for a hideout stood nearby.

After we gulped some water from jugs placed in the shade of a haystack by Dad and the other hay hands, Nonie, Bobby, and I rode our horses to Crouse Canyon. As we rode into the mouth of the canyon, we entered a fluorescent world of green boxelder trees and red rock walls. Listening to the rush of Crouse Creek echoing against the cliffs, we tried to imagine just where Charlie Crouse left the body of a teenager he was said to have killed so he could take his thoroughbred racehorse.

As we splashed in the creek, we kept watch for mountain lions and stinging nettles. Tracks were the most we ever saw of the mountain lions; when we brushed against the nettles, we hurried to slap creek mud on the spot to stop a blistering rash from spreading.

We rode back through the canyon entrance then stopped to get a drink from the spring that splattered onto a mossy boulder next to where the outlaw cabin once stood. An indentation in the ground, a couple of timbers, and some remnants of the foundation were all that remained of the building. Knowing that Dad had slipped on the large rock at the base of the spring and was laid up in a hospital in Salt Lake City for six weeks with a back injury, we were careful where we stepped. We took turns drinking from the aluminum tumbler kept there as we shed some of the sun's heat in the coolness of the green grass and bushes growing around the water.

Back in the saddle, we couldn't resist having a race, even though we were told not to run the horses wide-open unless we were working to turn a critter. We gave our horses their heads and dashed down a flat stretch of road. It wasn't easy for Bob to get Smokey shut down before the hay hands came into view. The white horse danced and pranced and puffed hard on the summer air, ready to take off in high gear if he got half a chance.

We rode across the hayfield and made our way to a mountain ridge just above the orchard to finish our horse corral. We'd already worked for days, dragging and stacking a ton of dead and twisted cedars in an impressive circle. Once we completed the corral we were only patient enough to leave our unsaddled horses in it for about fifteen minutes. After saddling up and riding east, we made an exciting discovery.

On a small rise at the edge of some cedars lay a manmade trench about five feet deep, six feet long, and three feet wide. Stacked to create a border, heavy flat rocks surrounded the top. Later that evening during supper, we sprinkled vinegar on beet greens and ladled brown gravy over slices of meat roasted with potatoes and carrots while telling the family about our find. The next day we all went to look it over.

Mom and Dad agreed, because of its design and location, it was very likely an outlaw lookout. Standing hidden in it with rifles resting on the rocks, men on the run would have had a far and sweeping view of the surrounding country while protected from the rear by the steep mountain. Or, they thought, it could have been constructed by Indians and used as a storage pit.

Evidence of countless Native American lifetimes lay across the ranch. Blackened earth where fires once gleamed, arrowheads, and all kinds of artifacts were scattered on ridges, over hills, and along sandy draws. For centuries, stirring chants and drums and the smell of pine and cedar smoke floated on the breezes as various tribes called this place home.

One day the three of us crossed a creek near the spring and went up the side of a steep climb, making our way through cedars, around brush, and over rocks. Nonie saw it first. There, attached to the hillside beneath a small ledge with a handprint still visible in its hardened mud, was a primitive oven made of rock and clay.

Endless mysteries and discoveries were all around us, waiting. In the light of day, and sometimes by the light of a buttermilk-colored moon, we followed trails or just our noses and searched.

Running back to the house from some outlying place, we liked stopping by Dad's shop. Haying season and equipment breakdowns always went together, and Dad was kept busy greasing and repairing machinery. Watching him weld a bar on the back of a tractor one day, we saw sparks spray in all directions.

"Now don't you kids look at this flame because it'll hurt your eyes," Dad warned. "And don't you dare touch this bar."

The moment Dad turned away, Nonie reached out and touched the innocent-looking metal bar. The split second of contact melted the prints from her fingers. Bobby and I watched her with big eyes, but we said nothing. We followed as she quickly made her way to the creek behind the shop. Sliding her hand into the coolness, she let the water carry the pain downstream. Ashamed, Nonie kept the injury hidden; none of us ever mentioned it.

One evening when the hay hands finished for the day, the usual alfalfa leaves, stems, and tiny slivers stuck to the sweat on their arms, around their necks, and even in the corners of their eyes. John Story, a dark-haired and good-looking cowboy, called out in a booming voice, "What's for supper, Ma Allen?"

We all loved this young man with the handsome smile who was back with us for the summer after serving three years in the Army. John became part of us years before when he lived and worked at the ranch. He delighted in teasing Mom, sometimes yanking the bow of her apron, setting it free. Talking her out of a quart jar of home-canned peaches, he gave her a wink as he whisked it off the pantry shelf and headed for the bunkhouse. Mom adored his playful nature and the talent he showed on the back of a horse. Her face lit up each time he called her "Ma" Allen.

"I'll have supper ready when you get back if all of you want to head to the river for a swim," Mom said.

Swimming and dog-paddling for an hour or so in the tepid water refreshed us and created huge appetites. When we returned to the house, the guys slicked down their hair in front of the mirror at the washstand on the porch, and the girls helped take up food from pots and skillets.

Supper was sweet and tender: fresh fried chicken stacked high on two large platters, garden peas and new potatoes in white sauce, grapes and chunks of peaches and pears mixed with lettuce and mayonnaise, and hot yeast rolls that had been dipped in melted butter before baking. Still warm from the oven and topped with hand-whipped cream, dessert was whole purple plums baked beneath a thick layer of vanilla cake.

As time moved beyond midsummer, apricots hung on branches, turning deep, sweet orange, and we ate them by the handful and the bowlful. The dark red baler with its big-fisted plunger ramming up and down, and tractors, mowers, and rakes continued from field to field doing their work. One afternoon Nonie convinced Dad to let her drive a small gray tractor the hundred or so yards to the shop. Bobby and I were eager to get in on that ride. After we climbed over the gears, we each perched on a fender.

Gripping the metal with both hands, we were focused on the roadway ahead when Nonie moved the lever downward, giving the tractor plenty of gas. She stood on the clutch pedal with one foot and the brake with the other, then moved the gearshift into place. The engine was revved, the transmission was in gear, and we were ready.

Then Nonie abruptly lifted both feet, simultaneously releasing the brake and clutch. Responding magnificently to having its clutch popped, the tractor reared and bucked forward. In one motion, both Bobby and I were flipped upside down, and only our hands grasping the fenders remained where they started.

Nonie was oblivious. She had no idea Bobby and I had switched ends and both were both dangling with our feet in the air and our noses nearly touching the churning tread on the big rear tires. She didn't see or hear Dad and John Story running behind, yelling. Submerged in the blare of the engine, she leaned forward, clutched the steering wheel with both hands, and aimed for the shop.

Out of the corner of her eye Nonie caught a glimpse of John. Turning her head toward him, she saw no color in his face as he wildly waved his arms. She stomped hard on the pedals and the tractor halted, nearly finishing the job of yanking Bobby and me loose.

Nonie started to cry as John reached for me and Dad grabbed Bobby to pull us upright. But we were not injured, and before long, with our bridles over our shoulders, we were laughing about our reckless ride. Jumping over a creek, we hurried across the pasture in search of our horses—and our next stunt.

It was a thrilling event once a year when our untamed breeding stock horse herd was brought in from the range downriver. Dad, John, and our teenaged brothers made an impressive sight on horseback, guiding the loping herd around the bend of the rocky hill.

"Find a place behind a tree where you can watch," Mom told us. "Now you kids know better than to move as they come by or you'll spook 'em."

Peeking around a fat cottonwood, we not only didn't move, we barely took a breath as the herd clattered along the cobblestones beside the house. The spring colts held their heads high and stayed close to their alert mothers. The adult horses snorted and watched with large eyes. Their manes, some silky and others in long knotted ringlets, floated with the rhythm of their gait.

Some of the horses soon wore a fresh Quarter Circle A brand. Young studs were gelded. A few horses were cut from the herd to be sold, and those chosen to be broke to ride were roped, haltered, and tied to corral posts where they were given feed and water. The rest of the herd ran and kicked up their heels as they dashed through the open gate, returning to their life of freedom.

It was a long process, getting a horse to neck rein and turn a cow on the run. Watching the cowboys from our spot next to Mom on top of the shed overlooking the stockade corral was better than almost anything.

The broncs were scared and the men usually a little nervous. As the horses trembled, their nostrils sucked air and snorted it out. Sometimes they reared back or struck with their front feet. The guys worked slowly, showing the horses that a human's touch and the feel of a saddle on their backs wasn't a cause for fear. They gently picked up the horses' feet and put them down and rubbed saddle blankets over their backs and rumps and down their legs. Speaking softly, the guys talked to their broncs and patted their foreheads. To teach the horses to lead, the men led them from the corral and off a small hill to the creek to drink several times a day.

Usually the first few times he got on the horse's back, the rider snubbed the bronc by tying its hackamore lead rope to the saddle horn of a gentle horse. The rider placed his foot in the stirrup to put his weight on one side and then the other of the bronc. At last the cowboy pulled himself up from the left side, swung his leg over, and settled into the saddle.

Led by the seasoned horse and its rider, a bronc's first steps were usually awkward until it grew accustomed to the weight. Sometimes the horses tried to rear and buck. But the snubbing process held their heads and kept horses and riders from getting hurt. The rider gave the lead rope more and more slack as the horse progressed. Before long the men were riding the horses in open country, teaching them to work cattle. The desired result was the creation of a dependable, hard-working partner. Sometimes, though, certain horses never lost the urge to buck.

We all took plenty of tumbles because of horses stumbling, saddles turning, or horses taking contrary notions. A small buckskin pinto mare that Nonie, Bobby, and I often rode had plenty of willful ideas. Her name was Sugar.

Sugar had a stop and go method: while loping she often stopped in her tracks, causing her rider to go—straight over her head. One spring after Sugar injured her knee, we made tea by steeping sagebrush leaves in hot water. We soaked her leg with the warm liquid several times a day for about a week. Although her lameness completely disappeared, her knee remained double its normal size. Her speed wasn't noticeably affected; neither was her temperament. Sugar could be gentle and as sweet as her name implied, but riding her was always risky business.

"Go to the cellar and get me about a half bucket of potatoes, Sissy," Mom told me.

I cringed. Going to the cellar had become my job and I knew the drill. Dug into a hillside next to the corral, the old cellar had two doors. The first led into a narrow walkway where cobweb drapes hung from its low ceiling. Behind the second door a rush of cool darkness waited to be released. Each time I went inside the cellar, the air was heavy with the smell of earth and sleeping vegetables and fruit. Walking bent over and dragging a five-gallon bucket, I always left plenty of room between me and the cobwebs or any other dreaded thing waiting to brush my hair from above.

Once I located the gunnysacks filled with potatoes I knew I could soon leave the cellar. But if the potatoes had begun to sprout, it took everything I had to stick my hand into those white, worm-like things. Hurrying to get it over with, I dropped the good-sized creatures into the metal bucket where they landed in a series of thuds.

Still crouching, I turned to leave as I dragged the heavy bucket behind me. Then I felt the breath of something horrible closing in on the back of my neck. Faster, faster I scurried, dragging the bucket until . . . daylight!

Suddenly the potatoes looked pleasant and plump. They smelled of the creek water, sunshine, and garden soil that created them. I happily lugged the bucket, half the size of me, up the hill and was enormously proud to hand it over to Mom.

I was imagining this entire routine when I took the bucket and started down the pathway leaving the yard. Sugar stood tied where I'd left her a few minutes earlier. Nonie and Bobby, riding their horses, disappeared behind the chicken coop.

Looking at Sugar, then the path to the cellar, I decided I might as well ride. After I led the mare beside the fence, I climbed on it so I could get both the bucket and me on her bare back. Settling comfortably, I held the reins in one hand and the bucket handle in the other. Tapping Sugar with my heels, I headed her toward the cellar.

I saw Nonie and Bobby come into sight just as Sugar detonated. Bucking with her head between her legs, the mare violently threw the clanging bucket and me off her back and bashed us against the side of the log icehouse.

When I woke up, Nonie was trying to pick me up from behind with her arms under my armpits. Completely limp and barely breathing, I slid like syrup down the front of her.

"Get up! You gotta get up!" Nonie begged. "Here comes Mom and she's on the warpath!"

"Yipes!" Bobby said. "Mom's pickin' up a club. Get her up!"

While on the run, Mom had grabbed a hefty tree branch from the ground just as she yelled something. Unable to make out what she was saying, Nonie heaved me upward but again my legs buckled.

Mom shouted again. "Leave her alone! Let her lie still till she gets her wind."

My daze was beginning to clear when Mom reached us. We all three thought we were going to get bopped with that branch. Instead, Mom hotfooted it over to Sugar and drew the leather reins over the mare's neck. We stood with our mouths open—we didn't often get to see our cowgirl mom in action.

Swinging up on Sugar's back, Mom kicked the sassy mare in the ribs and said, "Come on, try and lose me, you ole rip!" Then she smacked the branch across Sugar's rump. The mare humped her back and let out a long groan. It was plain she wanted to buck but didn't dare. Across the creek and up the road they went with Mom teaching Sugar more manners with every step.

It was an amazing turnaround for Sugar. She behaved herself quite well after she got her comeuppance from Mom. Mom and Dad would eventually give Sugar to some of our cousins, who took her home and loved her for many years.

⁘

As summer ripened, so did the apples in the orchard and the corn on the stalks. We picked giant tomatoes off garden vines and buckets of chokecherries and elderberries from bushes in Crouse Canyon. Kettles of apple butter simmered on the stove, and buttery juice ran to our elbows as kernels of corn popped between our teeth. But the sweet ripening also meant that our summer was ending.

Nonie, Bobby, and I walked in silence behind the two milk cows and their calves as we herded them slowly to the corral for the night. The sky was brilliant with colors spilling from the sun going down behind the peaks of Swallow Canyon. The trees, pastures, corrals, and mountains were aglow within its light. The air, heavy and sweet, smelled like a bowl of sugared strawberries. My eyes filled with tears because the next day Mom would drive us to Rock Springs and school would begin again.

⁘

Perhaps it was this awful, hollow feeling of leaving for the first time each fall that allowed the three of us to notice the gifts of nature and appreciate each moment spent on the ranch. How could we not wish for the summer to be never-ending? It had been perfect, and we had run free—as free as the wild colts doing pirouettes in the light of a buttermilk moon.

Top: *Bill and Lucille with a tractor stuck in the mud.*
Right: *Family friend and ranch hand, John D. Story as a teenager.*

Top: *John Story and Bobby Allen hunting sage chickens in 1956 on Cold Spring Mountain.*
Below: *Peacock strutting in front of the root cellar.*

Nina Taylor in the mid-1920s.

THE KILLDEER SANG LAST NIGHT

The first glimpse of the old mining town of Rock Springs made us moan. Because we were just displaced from cattle trails and the calls of pinyon jays, it seemed foreign. But as we drove along quiet, familiar streets, I felt some excitement about seeing Grandma Taylor and our town friends.

Grandma Taylor, Mom's mother, lived a short distance away from our house. Mom and I often walked hand in hand to her place. Grandma's tidy home almost always smelled pleasantly of brewing tea, stewed prunes, and toast. The large oval-framed black and white photographs on the walls and the lawyer-style oak bookcase were partial reminders of the decor of her once beautiful ranch house.

It made me sad that Grandpa Taylor died in 1946, three years before I was born. He was said to be an extraordinary man.

Our grandparents, Charles Melvin "C.M." and Nina Taylor, and their two children, five-year-old Jesse and two-year-old Nancy, first arrived in Brown's Park from Ainsworth, Nebraska, in a covered wagon in 1906. Until a few days before their arrival, they had never heard of the valley that was to become their home.

Farming in Nebraska and long dreaming of having a cattle ranch within the mountains, Grandpa corresponded with the postmasters in Rangely, Colorado, and Vernal, Utah, about life in that part of the country. Before long, Grandpa and Grandma sold their farm, many of their belongings, and all their livestock except for the gray team and bay saddle horse they would need for their journey.

Sorry to leave family and friends and a little frightened of the unknown, they were nonetheless excited and resolute to go west.

After several weeks of adventurous travel, it was a broken, washed-out bridge that changed their path. Standing on the bank of the Yampa River, they could see the tiny town of Maybell, Colorado, but they couldn't ford the river with the wagon to get there.

Basin big sagebrush can grow many feet tall. Within the shelter of these gray and fragrant bushes the family made camp. The next morning, Grandpa borrowed a rowboat and made his way to Maybell to seek some advice. While he was gone, Grandma was startled when two men rode suddenly out of the brush. Though the men were watchful and seemed on edge, they treated Grandma with respect and stayed only long enough for a quick cup of coffee and some biscuits. As they rode away, one of the men turned in his saddle and said, "Since you folks can't get across the river, you might think about heading toward Brown's Hole." Although she would never know for sure, she was convinced the men were outlaws on the run, and Grandma was very relieved when Grandpa returned.

Supper began to steam and sizzle on the fire. Grandpa hadn't found any solutions in Maybell, and the young couple was still undecided about what to do when a cowboy named Bill Braggs rode in, leading two packhorses and an extra saddle horse. He was made welcome.

"Why, yes," he said. "I know Brown's Hole, or Brown's Park. People call it both. Anyway, that's where I've just come from. I graze cattle there, sometimes."

The adults stayed up late, talking about the ranching valley of Brown's Park.

When they parted company the next morning, it was Bill Braggs' directions they were following when they made noon camp on a grassy meadow just above a bridge on Snake River. As Grandma brought out a two-gallon wooden keg of herring and a plate of biscuits, Grandpa watched some cowboy activity upriver. Three cowhands were working more cattle than he had ever seen in one herd.

One of the riders reined away from the others and came on a trot to the Taylor wagon. Dressed in chaps and a hat, an attractive woman with dark red hair and greenish-gray eyes stepped easily from her horse.

Ann Bassett Bernard happily shared their midday meal. When she learned they were on their way to Brown's Park, she spilled over with stories of the valley she loved. She gave them final directions, wished them well, and rode her horse at a lope back to her work.

Grandpa and Grandma would remain friends with this top-notch cowhand for many years. They would learn she was the first white child born in Brown's Park. In 1913, they, along with everyone else, began calling her "Queen Ann" after a Denver newspaper reporter labeled her "Queen of the Cattle Rustlers" because of her ongoing battles with Ora Haley of the massive Two-Bar Ranch.

A couple of days later, the covered wagon moved to the top of a rise, and Grandpa, Grandma, Jesse, and Nancy looked upon the quiet beauty of Brown's Park. To their distant right was Irish Canyon, close on the left were the high cliffs of the mouth of Lodore Canyon where the Green River passes out of the valley. Diamond Mountain and Cold Spring Mountain formed the sides of the valley and each crinkled westward in stunning shades of blue.

When the covered wagon finally creaked to a halt, it was next to the bunkhouse and beneath the shade of the cottonwood trees at Bridgeport, Utah, in upper Brown's Park. Located next to the river, Bridgeport was closely surrounded by mountains and three canyon entries into the valley.

Bridgeport was a stopping point for Native American families traveling between reservations. Tepees and other types of camps were scattered along the river. Indian children ran and giggled, gray smoke curled skyward from many small fires, and a herd of colorful horses stood in the main corral.

Charlie Crouse and his wife, Mary, had sold the Brown's Park Livestock Ranch a few years earlier, and Charlie tried his hand at running a saloon in Vernal, Utah, where some of his best customers were his outlaw friends, including Butch Cassidy. But he soon moved back to Brown's Park to some acreage he owned near the river. He had a toll bridge built to connect the north side of the river with the south as he worked at establishing Bridgeport. Before long the place had a main house; bunkhouse; a combination post office, store, and saloon; a blacksmith shop; a set of corrals; and a dugout cellar sometimes used for lodging. By the time Grandpa and Grandma arrived in 1906, the young bridge had already been destroyed by a rampaging ice jam. Because of the death of his wife, Mary, in 1904, Charlie did not have the heart to rebuild it. He had stopped selling just about everything except liquor, and he kept quite a bit of that supply for himself. But he was a very good and helpful friend to the Taylor family.

A new life filled with promise began for Grandpa, Grandma, and their children after arriving at Bridgeport. Grandpa went to work for Charlie Crouse the next day cleaning river trash from a large irrigation ditch. Grandpa and Grandma soon made solid friendships with several individuals who would become historic figures, including Charlie Crouse and John Jarvie. John Jarvie's ranch, store, and ferry operation sat just a short distance upriver from Bridgeport and had been there since the early 1880s.

Grandpa and Grandma soon made a deal with Charlie Crouse to buy a beautiful homestead he owned, where Charlie's half brother, Joe Tolliver, once lived with his wife and children. Still called the Joe Tolliver place, the house and corrals sat snug against the foot of Diamond Mountain. Among cedars, creeks, pines, hay meadows, and tall stands of cottonwood, the Taylors started building their ranch. Grandpa took jobs hauling freight for both Charlie Crouse and John Jarvie and did whatever else he could to make money to invest in a cattle herd. In 1907, Grandpa and Grandma purchased the old Dr. Parsons place from John Jarvie. Located near the river, and adjoining the Joe Tolliver place, it added considerably to the size of what was now the Taylor Ranch.

Grandma and Grandpa learned from Charlie Crouse that Joe Tolliver was the fellow who stabbed and killed cowboy Charlie Seger during a poker game in the kitchen of what became our ranch home.

Joe Tolliver was a drinker and often found trouble. He eventually moved to Vernal, Utah, and went to work as a deputy sheriff. He apparently made a pretty good lawman when he was sober. One day, he went to a barbershop and lounged back in the chair to get a shave. Tolliver made the barber nervous when he kept taking his revolver from its holster. When the barber spoke up that he was worried someone was going to get hurt, Joe Tolliver, for an unknown reason, brought the gun up to his own temple, pulled the trigger, and instantly ended his life.

A part of Charlie Crouse was still the bold youngster who endured the rigors of serving in the Civil War, hauling freight and fighting Indians on the Great Plains, and settling a young frontier, all in his own way. He was a loyal friend and, for the most part, a positive force in Brown's Park. He was the father of three children who he insisted be properly educated. But he had been a hard man, had witnessed death at an early age, and had killed, more than once. Nearing the end of his life, he was a heavy-hearted and sorrowful man.

More and more often when Charlie Crouse went to see Grandpa and Grandma, he sat on the fireplace hearth, liquor jug at his side, and talked about his life. He had never imagined anything would happen to his Mary; for so many years he had taken her comforting presence for granted.

"My goodness, Taylor," he would tell Grandpa. "I had a good woman and I treated her bad." Then he'd drink deeply from his whiskey jug until he passed out. He also talked to Grandpa about Joe Tolliver's suicide in Vernal. "I always accused Joe of having no nerve," he said. "You know, I believe he had more nerve than any of us. I've tried to kill myself a dozen times."

Before long, Charlie Crouse gave up Bridgeport and went to live with his daughter, Minnie, at her Wyoming homestead several miles northwest of Brown's Park on Spring Creek. The last time he came to visit, he gave Uncle Jesse his pearl-handled pocketknife. Not long after, Charlie Crouse became ill while traveling to Rock Springs alone in a buggy. A neighbor, Pete Dorrence, found him slumped across the seat. Pete took Charlie home with him where Charlie soon passed away.

❧

By their third fall at the Tolliver place, Grandma and Grandpa had planted asparagus and lilacs next to the creek and some fruit trees beside the garden. Jesse and Nancy were rarely more than a few feet apart as they ran and played. But when five-year-old Nancy contracted scarlet fever, it quickly overtook and killed her.

With a November chill in the air, Grandpa steadied his hands and built a pine coffin. Nancy was buried beneath some tall cottonwoods where the small mound barely showed above the fallen leaves.

The despair left by Nancy's death was severe: Grandpa grieved deeply but found comfort in the mountains, streams, and wildlife of the valley. He squared his shoulders and allowed the joy he found in life to return. Grandma recovered from her own bout with scarlet fever, but as she grieved for Nancy, she felt a seed of bitterness toward the valley take root. Jesse, now eight years old, grieved and discovered that his and Nancy's hiding places and the shadows among the cedars were frightening to him now. He found no joy in walking beside the creek or in smelling his mother's baking coffee cakes. He felt alone. It was a feeling he never got over—not for the rest of his life.

Grandpa and Grandma Taylor's next child, Bessie, was a beautiful but fragile girl who was born deaf. Mom, who was their final child, was two weeks old in 1915 when she rode in a buckboard in Grandma's arms as Grandpa guided the team off Diamond Mountain through Sears Canyon and into Brown's Park. By then they had moved closer to the river on Sears Creek to the part of their ranch known as the Parsons place.

Home for the Taylors on Sears Creek was a three-room log cabin that was the oldest existing building in that part of the country. Each room had a front door, but the cabin had no adjoining doors inside. Built in the 1870s by Dr. John D. Parsons, who was a medical doctor, postmaster, and ferry operator, it was later used by a variety of people, including outlaws Butch Cassidy and his friend Matt Warner. At the springhouse near the Parsons' cabin, Warner's wife, Rose, fell and severely injured her leg.

Willard E. Christiansen, alias Matt Warner, owned a ranch on Diamond Mountain. He had an outlaw career that carried across several states. After rustling cattle on a large scale, his first bank robbery was with Butch Cassidy at Telluride, Colorado. Running from the law, the outlaws made it to the Brown's Park Livestock Ranch where they were given shelter by their friend, Charlie Crouse, in the cabin by the spring a ways from the ranch house. Warner was eventually captured, and while he was in prison, his wife, whose leg had never healed after her fall at the Parsons place, died of bone cancer. Warner later received a pardon and went on to live an honest life.

Mom adored their home on Sears Creek. She learned all the duties of running a household. But she was at her best riding horseback beside her dad, who always called her "Babe."

Grandpa was described to me as "tough and rugged as a wild horse, yet a handsome and gentle man." Most who knew him, including the neighboring children, thought him to be a gallant figure. When he returned from trips, he always brought treats the likes of which they rarely saw—oranges, graham crackers, or a dandy gift such as a silver ring or a set of toy pistols.

As Mom grew up, many times upon the valley's silken air she heard both the voice of her father calling out and the cracking report of his bullwhip as he worked his cattle. Again and again the sounds carried across sagebrush slopes and cedar groves as Mom rode with her dad, who was by then one of the area's most respected cattlemen.

Grandpa rode an A-fork saddle on the back of his cow horses. Over his brown-checkered Pendleton pants he wore black batwing chaps. His boots, made in Olathe, Kansas, were high-heeled and high-topped with mule ears and plenty of stitching and inlay. On his left foot he wore a silver-mounted G.S. Garcia spur. When questioned about wearing only one spur, he replied: "Oh, if you spur one side, the other'n'll come along." Wearing a ten-gallon Stetson, he laughed and said: "The bigger the hat, the better the hand. But I'll never hire a man who wears a straw hat or rolls his own cigarettes. If he's not workin' on a smoke, he's chasin' his hat!"

Besides being active in better range interests and management, Grandpa was also a conservationist. He loved all forms of wildlife and surrounded himself with them. He introduced pheasants to the valley and grinned when he heard them throughout the day. He admired the Canada geese as they flew overhead and landed in his fields. He brought peacocks to his ranch and came to love the calls they made from their roosts in the tall cottonwoods. In Colorado he bought buffalo—six heifers and two bulls. For his little buffalo herd he built a six-strand wire fence around a large pasture near the house.

Grandpa wasn't successful in getting quail to flourish, and the bullfrogs he released never sang in the summer evenings. But the nearby pond at Salt Springs, which he preserved and protected, was a wonderful home for whooping cranes, blue herons, ducks, and wild swans. Besides being a protected place from hunters, the pond was near a natural salt lick, which drew all sorts of wildlife from deer to badgers.

One day a pushy little man stopped by and began asking directions to the Salt Springs pond. The man was aghast when Grandpa, sitting on a dappled gray gelding named Coon, told the man that hunting wasn't allowed at the pond.

"Mr. Taylor, I don't believe you know to whom you're talking. I happen to be a church preacher from Craig, Colorado, and I insist that I be able to go duck hunting!"

Grandpa looked down at the man and slowly took his bullwhip from its coiled nest around the saddle horn. Calmly he said, "I don't care if you are the Christ Jesus from Heaven, you're not hunting my pond." Although the preacher's face reddened, he didn't speak. Instead he spun around and stomped away. For many years the wildlife of Brown's Park benefited from Grandpa's protection and from his fruit trees and alfalfa and grain fields.

Growing up, Mom loved the springhouse and the way wild roses completely covered the small log building. Inside, icy water came up from the ground in tiny, constant bubbles. A dipper for getting drinks hung on a nail, and pails of milk were placed on submerged rock shelves where the water almost reached their tops. The milk, along with butter and three-gallon crockery jars filled with cream, was kept deliciously cold. Other foods were kept fresh in the springhouse as well, including a fifty-gallon barrel of salted-down cucumbers from which Grandma made sweet pickles all winter long and large crockery jars filled with sausage patties layered with waxy grease to seal in freshness.

Indian families traveling back and forth to their reservations often camped nearby. Grandpa respected them and their beliefs and taught Mom to do the same. She watched through the fence as fires lit their campgrounds and flickered against the tepees. The children befriended her, and as she ran and played with the happy kids, the women stayed busy preparing food and doing chores. Mom loved these visitors and wished they could stay camped along the sandy ridges in the cedars, the way their ancestors had.

When Mom was about eleven, construction on a new home began. Grandpa hauled the lumber from Ruple's Sawmill on Diamond Mountain. On the days her dad was going after lumber, Mom hopped out of bed at the first sound of movement so she could be ready to leave by four. The trip to the sawmill took them up the Old Place Draw where the wagon wheels left behind rust-colored marks on the rocks. They traveled through Sears Canyon to the top of the mountain and on to Pot Creek. The constant rhythm of the wagon wheels, the jangle of the harness, and the clap of hooves always lulled Mom to sleep.

When the beautiful new home was completed, it had hardwood floors, three bedrooms, a kitchen, a dining room, a living room, and a bathroom with a pretty-legged bathtub and a kerosene water heater. The walls were painted in various pastel shades. Grandma made attractive designs on some of them by dipping large rags in paint, wringing the excess out, and then rolling them along the walls to form patterns. Grandma and Grandpa hung family portraits in large oval frames as soon as the paint was dry.

There was a large, black cookstove in the kitchen, plenty of cupboards, a coffee grinder hooked to a worktable, and a roomy pantry with lots of shelves. Meals were eaten on the oak dining table near a bay window filled with clusters of red geranium blossoms. A buffet and china closet gleamed nearby.

The mantle over the brick fireplace in the living room held an intricately carved clock that chimed on the hour. In the corner stood the oak bookcase. Sometimes in the evenings, by the light of wall-mounted glass kerosene lamps, Mom and Bessie embroidered or did tatting while Grandpa and Grandma read from their collection of books. Occasionally, Grandma played her silver harmonica or the oak piano.

Off the kitchen and dining room was a large, screened porch. There was a rack on the porch wall for Grandpa's guns and a worktable for Grandma. On the table, Grandma kept a crock of clabbered milk covered with a piece of cheesecloth. She used the milk for baking and also enjoyed eating the curds and whey.

Outside, a pie cherry tree was usually full of robins in the summer as the tree spread shade across the porch and kitchen. Along with a variety of apple and crab apple trees, there were pear, black cherry, peach, apricot, and plum trees. In the spring, the fragrant lilac and fruit blossoms perfumed the air. The iris plants grew tall and flowered in elegant colors. Columbines, transplanted from the mountain, bloomed beneath the kitchen window. The many flowering bushes and plants were irresistible to nectar-loving creatures, including a large family of hummingbirds.

The yard fence had pretty wire gates with vine-covered arches above them. The entire front area sweeping away from the house was in lawn. Grandpa kept the grass short and groomed with a horse-drawn mower.

When Grandpa announced he was going to have one of his oyster stew and cracker suppers, neighbors showed up on horseback and in wagons. Grandpa did the cooking and kept dipping in and filling bowls with steaming soup made of milk, oysters, butter, salt, and pepper until everyone was full. Then the men usually headed to the corrals to visit, and the kids ran to play along the creek while the women chatted and washed the dishes.

To attend the dances at the Lodore School, where young and old kicked up their heels and swayed to the rhythm of the music, the Taylor family traveled all day in a horse-drawn wagon. Listening to the beauty of the violin, Grandpa said, "If Brown's Park could sing, it would sound just like that ole fiddle."

In 1931, our dad moved to Brown's Park and went to work for Grandpa. He and Mom courted, then were married September 22, 1932, which was shortly after Mom's sister Bessie married Wilson Garrison.

Uncle Wilson and Aunt Bessie were very happy together and soon had a baby boy named Melvin. On the first day of June 1936, Wilson was away, checking cattle at their summer range on Cold Spring Mountain. He knew Bessie wasn't feeling well and had left her and Melvin in the care of Grandma while he went to the mountain.

Decades later, Uncle Wilson told me the whole story. It was early morning and he was saddling his black cow horse, Peanuts, preparing to drive the cattle out of the timber and away from the poisonous purple larkspur when he saw his good friend, Bob Teters, suddenly come loping out of the trees.

"Charlie Taylor sent me to get you, Wilson. Bessie's taken a turn for the worse. You better hurry."

A few minutes later, the two men and their horses raced over brush and new sprouts of grass. Before long Bob Teters pulled up on his horse, yelling to Wilson that his horse was worn out and for Wilson to go ahead.

Wilson spurred Peanuts into a gallop and pushed the gelding hard across meadows, down steep grades, over hills, through gullies and draws, and along sagebrush-covered flats. Finally, Wilson pulled the winded and sweat-soaked gelding to a stop near the Taylor house; then he jumped from the saddle and ran.

Just before he got to the yard gate, he saw Dr. Arbogast from Rock Springs step out of the screened porch. Wilson stopped. A tingling sensation spread across his shoulders, down into his stomach, and rushed in a wave down his legs, leaving them numb. The doctor's voice was soft. "She's gone," he said.

Uncle Wilson learned that Aunt Bessie had died before the doctor arrived. "She had scarlet fever, Wilson," the doctor told him. "The glands in her throat were so swollen that they closed it off. It wouldn't have mattered if there'd been a dozen doctors here. There is nothing that could have been done."

Just as Grandma had with her little Nancy, she had worked tirelessly to do everything she could for Bessie. Now she had given up two of her beautiful daughters to scarlet fever—and to Brown's Park.

On June 3, 1936, the very day Bessie was buried, Mom, also suffering from scarlet fever, gave birth to her first child. When little Lucille Marie struggled her way into the world, her skin was fiery red, but she was healthy and strong.

Uncle Wilson's grief consumed him. Once happy-natured, he became quiet and brooding. Agreeing it was best for his son, he gave Melvin to Grandma and Grandpa to raise. He quit ranching soon after and moved to Rock Springs where he spent the rest of his life.

In 1943, Grandpa was telling stories to Lucille and Melvin while he worked near the riverbank. Uncle Jesse and his family lived on the other side of the river, and Grandpa was building a footbridge that would be a safe way for his grandchildren to cross. While he listened to the flow of the river and the giggles of playing children, a stroke suddenly sent Grandpa tumbling to the ground.

After the initial stroke, Grandpa and Grandma knew they had to leave the valley and move to town. Grandpa sold his buffalo herd and watched as they were slaughtered for meat. He tried to decide what to take and what to leave and ached with saying good-bye to his fruit trees and the saddle horses that had served him so well. He leaned against a corral post and looked over his pretty place, at the home and all the buildings he built when his hands were strong. He lifted his eyes to the mountains, the ones that called to him so long ago. To them and to his old love, Brown's Park, he bid farewell.

Shortly after Grandma and Grandpa moved to Rock Springs, Mom and Dad bought a home nearby so the kids could attend school and Mom could be near to help her mother and dad as much as possible.

When Grandpa died in 1946, after a series of strokes totally paralyzed him, Mom's world could never be the same. But he had given her his character, so she continued to work hard and love life the way he taught her. Mom showed us Grandpa's bullwhip. It had a long, hickory handle attached to fifteen feet of braided rawhide with a buckskin popper on the end. I longed to know this man.

Mom was devastated when Grandma said the words, "No, I won't sell the ranch to you and I won't sell it to anyone who will!" Instead Grandma sold the beautiful Taylor Ranch, along with Grandpa's dinner bell, the wagons, harnesses, machinery, and everything else, to a man named Harold Calder from Bountiful, Utah. Mom never understood why. Perhaps it was because her mother had already given up two of her daughters to the ranch. Whatever Grandma's reason, Mom accepted it. She and Dad carried their ranching dreams forward on the Brown's Park Livestock Ranch and watched the steady decline of the Taylor Ranch. All the while, Mom remained devoted to her mother.

Grandma usually treated us with cool reserve, rarely showing affection. Another blow to Grandma, further hardening her, came in 1957, in a telegram from the Army, that Melvin, her handsome grandson whom she had built her entire world around, had been killed in a car accident.

I spent a lot of time with Grandma in her immaculate home, obeying her strict routine. I accepted the way she sat in silence for long periods either looking out the window or reading magazines and papers, ignoring me. But I loved the rare moments when she laughed with her hand cupped over her nose and mouth, then talked about my mother as a child. I treasured the one time that she spoke about the Taylor Ranch, telling me softly how the killdeer sang at night.

⤢

As Mom drove down the gravel roadway of our street that Sunday in September, friends ran to greet us. Our neighborhood was much like a cottontail lair where the young scurried out at dusk to romp. I saw Barbara Francis, my best friend. She always ignored my shyness and insisted I ignore it, too. And skipping across the street came Kaylou Muir and her little brother, Louie. Sometimes they all went with us to the ranch. They loved it there.

In this different world, we loved going to the movies, riding bikes, getting fountain drinks and banana splits at the drugstore lunch counter, and hearing the "clackity" rhythm of passing trains. We enjoyed the good things Rock Springs offered, but only because Mom was always close by to soothe, listen, and be our buffer against the difficult, sometimes painful, challenges of being country kids trying to fit in and thrive in a school in town.

Nonie, Bobby, and I helped unload the car then rushed among our friends to play kick-the-can. I swallowed the lump of sadness I had held in my throat since we left the ranch. I was happy. I knew five days would soon pass. Then we could return to the place where the songs of lakes and creeks blended with those of the killdeer, and we'd hear them, long into the night.

Top left: *Nina Taylor in 1901.*
Top right: *C.M. Taylor in 1901*
Middle: *The C.M. Taylor family in 1906 on the day they were heading west from Nebraska. Shown are C.M., Nina, Nancy, and Jesse.*
Left: *C.M. at the Taylor Ranch about 1930.*

Left: *C.M. wearing his buffalo-hide coat.*
Below right: *Marie with her sister, Bessie, at the Taylor Ranch.*
Below left: *The Taylor children, Bessie, Marie, and Jesse, in 1929.*

Left: *Bill and Marie's wedding photo, September 22, 1932. Shown are Bessie Garrison, Marie, Bill, and Bessie's husband, Wilson Garrison.*

Below: *Bill and C.M. preparing for a cattle drive to Rock Springs, Wyoming, about 1938.*

Top: *Marie on a cliff above the river in 1931 at the Taylor Ranch.*

Right: *C.M. and Nina at the Taylor Ranch, about 1935.*

The Brown's Park Livestock Ranch,
taken from the swinging bridge.

WHEN THE RIVER SPOKE

The river was running ice by mid-December. Had it been free of ice or frozen solid, we could have crossed the cattle at the mouth of Swallow Canyon and had them home in half a day. As it was, we had to trail them a long distance to get across on the swinging bridge.

The cows and their calves had spent the summer chewing mouthfuls of grass on the summer range in Colorado on Cold Spring Mountain. After the herd was trailed down to Brown's Park in October, the calves were loaded in trucks and shipped from the corrals on Bake Oven Flat to Craig, Colorado. From there they were shipped by train to the Denver market. The mother cows were then pushed a short distance upriver and left to graze on the range spreading from the mouth of Red Creek Canyon. We called the area the Bradshaw place, after a family who once lived there. Now the feed was short and it was time to bring the cows home for the winter where they would be fed hay and pellets of cow cake.

Dad always treated the river with respect. He relied on it to say where or when we could cross.

❧

"It takes two to three inches of ice to hold a man," Dad told us. "Four inches'll hold a horse, but ten inches could probably hold a freight train. If the ice ever sounds dull or makes a thudding sound when you put some weight on it, you stay off it because that means it's rotten. But if it sings, making sharp cracking noises zinging in different directions, that means it's good ice." He shook his finger. "But you need to chop a hole down through it with an axe to be safe, and then you'll know. You can trust it if it's thick enough. Once when a big bunch of our cattle got to milling about halfway across, the ice bowed way up in the center, but it held them."

�֍

It was Saturday morning and heavy frost glistened across the December dawn in 1955 as Dad, Nonie, Bobby, and I rode our horses from the corrals on Bake Oven Flat.

Before we left home that morning, Mom helped me rummage through the box she kept filled with hand-me-down ranch gloves. Getting a right and left glove was pretty important. But if they matched, that was a bonus. I happily stuffed a pair of mittens in my coat pocket as Mom tugged a warm hat down over my ears. Bobby's old boots fit me just right with my two pairs of socks.

Charlie was now a senior in high school and both he and Les were busy in Rock Springs with school activities. That left the three of us to help Dad bring the cows home. By the time we got the cattle gathered out of the cedars and off the sagebrush hills and flats of the Bradshaw, it was snowing.

I had turned six over the summer and was certainly capable of making an all day ride. But sitting in a classroom all day five days a week had softened my constitution. Cold passed through the layers of clothing and caused all my movable parts to stiffen. Going to the bathroom was really a ridiculous notion. But the need was building, and it was relentless.

On the hill above the Jarvie place, I couldn't wait any longer to find a spot behind a cedar. When I slid from the saddle, my boots hit the ground with a jolt and pain surged through my cold feet. After hobbling behind a bushy tree, I pulled off my mittens and tried to yank on the button and zipper of my pants, but my fingers were flimsy. I jigged and danced. The urge was ready to conquer the moment when, finally, my britches came loose. Blessed relief!

Moments later, I peeked around the branches and squinted to see through the storm. I stood helpless. If getting my pants undone was difficult, getting them buttoned and zipped again was impossible. I spotted Nonie as she went off the hill and out of sight. I yelled her name as tears of frustration burned my eyes and coated the sound of my voice.

Up and over the steep bank, Nonie and her horse clambered through the rocks. In an instant she was there, just as I always counted on her to be. Standing behind me and reaching around my middle, she pulled on my denim pants and forced her frigid hands to respond. Once she got me girded up and back in the saddle, we trotted side by side and fell in behind the herd. We were three quarters of a day away from home. No matter how cold it got, we had to keep at it and move forward.

The cows knew where they were going, so they lined out and stepped along at a lively pace. Their backs were coated with snow, and steam came from their nostrils. I watched Dad rein his horse along the side of a hill and could scarcely believe the sight of him. As he wore a cowboy hat, it wasn't unusual that nothing was over his ears, but it was incredible to me that he didn't even have his coat buttoned! I felt like the bird I just saw sitting on a bush. The little thing had its feathers ruffled and its head pulled back and tucked into its shoulders. As we passed beside the old corrals and buildings of the Jarvie Ranch nestled near the bank of the river, Dad seemed unaware of any cold sliding down the back of his neck.

When he went to the front of the herd to join Bobby, I asked Nonie, "Did you see Dad with his coat wide-open?"

Shivering, she nodded and said, "He's a tough man."

Both the Bradshaw and Jarvie places were part of our ranch. Mom and Dad and their older kids once lived at the Jarvie. Here Dad's redheaded uncle, Charlie Green, secretly built a still in the bunkhouse. It caught fire and burned the building to the ground, taking with it Mom's wedding dress and stacks of old photographs.

As we moved the cattle alongside the Jarvie pasture, I noticed the rusty barbed wire still held several tin cans from the early days. Filled with small rocks, they were meant to clank when the wire was disturbed and frighten predators away from the livestock.

The John Jarvie Ranch was once a thriving business. Moving here in 1880, Jarvie, a Scottish immigrant, along with his wife, Nell, and their four boys, ran a store, post office, and ferry. Stagecoaches arriving by way of Red Creek Canyon stopped here before crossing the river and making their way over Diamond Mountain. Travelers and locals found John Jarvie, who spoke with a strong

Scottish accent, to be not only a rancher and storekeeper but a scholar as well. He was admired, respected, and loved by scores of people in the surrounding three-state area.

When Grandma and Grandpa Taylor moved nearby, a close friendship quickly grew between them and John Jarvie. By then Nell had died, and the Jarvie boys—John Jr., Tom, Archie, and Jimmy—were living away from home. Jarvie often challenged young Jesse Taylor to a foot race before bounding away through the sagebrush like a deer. In winter John Jarvie made a marvelous sight to all by gliding along the frozen river on ice skates with his long white hair and beard blowing in the breeze.

On July 6, 1909, Grandma, in her sixth month of pregnancy with Bessie, was home at the Tolliver place. Grandpa, then working for Martin Whalen as foreman of the Brown's Park Livestock Ranch, was busy in the hayfields with another hired man, Gordon Wilson. Uncle Jesse and his friend, Walter Hanks, Jr., were nearby hunting rabbits.

As the sun was setting behind King's Point, Grandpa looked up and saw ranch hand Bill Lookingbill riding hard toward them.

After bringing his horse to a stop, Lookingbill said, "It's old man Jarvie, fellas. Somethin' bad has happened. I just saw Nina over at the Tolliver. She said Jimmy Jarvie had come to the house wanting a gun. Nina said he was in an awful state and she was afraid to give him one. She said Jimmy told her he thinks somebody has robbed and killed his dad!"

⁂

Word that John Jarvie and the rowboat he kept at the river were missing and that his home and store had been ransacked spread quickly throughout the valley. By morning most of the Jarvie boys and a sizable crowd of ranchers and ranch hands had gathered at the Brown's Park Livestock Ranch. Almost all of them had their guns, but they were confounded that they had very little ammunition between them. Nonetheless, Grandpa and the other men formed a posse and got ready to head to the Jarvie Ranch. Uncle Jesse, now eight years old, begged to go along. When the men rode out, Uncle Jesse followed behind riding an old mare that neighbor Adam Davenport loaned him.

From the Jarvie house, the men followed a trail of blood and drag marks leading to the river. Along the way, they saw strands of white hair snagged on bushes. The river revealed much of the story: impressions in the damp sand along the bank showed where Jarvie's body had lain, even showing the pattern of the rivets in his pants and what was feared to be a hole in the back of his head.

As they pieced clues together, the ranchers became certain that the identity of one of the killers was a man they all knew and none liked: George Hood. The day before, Harold King and his wife had seen Hood and another man they didn't recognize walk out of the mouth of nearby Jesse Ewing Canyon and head toward the Jarvie place.

Emotions were raw among the ranchers. "To hell with the law! After we capture those two birds, we'll strip 'em and put 'em naked in the willows at the Park Live. We'll leave the buggers there for the mosquitoes to eat on until they confess. And when they do admit to it, by damn, we'll hang 'em from the ferry cable post!"

Grandpa and the other ranchers surmised that the two men were still in the area and planning to steal some horses because they had taken several ropes and pairs of hobbles from Jarvie's store. But as they tracked the men, they found the ropes and hobbles abandoned part way up a draw just below Bridgeport.

The tracks showed that the two had not stayed in Brown's Park but had left by way of Jesse Ewing Canyon. The group of ranchers halted at the red mouth of the steep canyon. They realized the opportunities for being caught in an ambush on the roadless climb were endless. That, coupled with their shortage of ammunition, made pursuit into the canyon foolhardy. Instead, John Jarvie, Jr. decided to go alone to notify the sheriff in Rock Springs, traveling through Red Creek Canyon on the road rather than risking Jesse Ewing Canyon. The rest of the men rode back to John Jarvie's home and hurriedly built a raft. They dragged the river but found nothing.

The two killers, who did turn out to be George Hood and his brother-in-law, Bill McKinnley, had luck on their side, and it stayed there. Before the law got the chance to react, the murderers got away on an eastbound train.

Eight days after the murder and more than twenty miles downstream, John Jarvie was found where the river chose to leave him. Archie Jarvie discovered his father's overturned rowboat and found his father's body still tied fast in the boat by a piece of clothesline. Because one of John's arms had come free and had tangled tight in a clump of willows, the boat was moored. If not for the willows, the river current would have soon swept the boat into the mouth of Lodore Canyon and into the fury of the river's white water rapids.

Now that the body was found, a more complete picture of the crime could be formed. After sharing a meal with John Jarvie, the two men, intent on robbery, apparently struck him on the head. When the old man ran outside, he was shot in the back between the shoulders. Then at close range, he was shot through the temple. John was then dragged by his heels on a path around the house, across the west step, out the west gate, and past the front of the dugout cellar, where he and Nell had made their first home. His lifeless body was dumped into the rowboat and tied in by the piece of clothesline. Then the rope holding the boat was cut and the boat set adrift. The men then ransacked the house and store and took what they wanted.

John had recently been to Rock Springs to make his deposits, so not much money was in the safe. Although Hood and McKinnley missed a cigar box full of change on the shelf, they didn't miss the trunk where John kept some personal items, including his pearl-handled pistol.

As the law pursued the killers, it was discovered that George Hood got off the train for a short stop at Point of Rocks east of Rock Springs. There he pawned a new pair of shoes and a pearl-handled six-shooter. He also was heard to ask if anyone could change a one hundred dollar bill.

Two five-hundred-dollar rewards for information leading to the arrest of the killers were established. One was from the people of Rock Springs, the other from Governor Cutler of Utah. Regardless, Hood and McKinnley had vanished.

Grandpa, Grandma, and other friends sadly worked together to put John's plundered home back in some sort of order. They discovered Nell's possessions sitting on the dresser top and her clothes still hanging in the closet where they had remained since her death from tuberculosis in 1895.

When the law had no success in finding Hood and McKinnley, Jimmy and Archie Jarvie made a vow to bring their father's murderers to justice. They tried so hard. But Archie was killed in a suspicious coal mining accident when the search took them to Idaho. Jimmy stayed on their trail and followed the killers to the eastern United States and back to Jackson Hole, Wyoming, and then to Pocatello, Idaho. From there, devastating word came that someone had pushed Jimmy from a second floor hotel window. The fall broke his neck and he died instantly. The vow was, forever, unfulfilled.

⌘

As we rode by the old Jarvie place, and the snow fell softly upon the weathered posts and buildings, the place did not have a feeling of sadness to me. It was much too pretty for that.

About a mile down the road, we arrived at the ruins of Bridgeport, the place established by Charlie Crouse just before the turn of the last century.

Trailing our cattle through snowy sagebrush and greasewood, we rode by the old dugout. Its sturdy skeleton was about all that was left of the buildings. Old and wrinkled bark surrounded the mighty cottonwoods as the trees stood reaching high into the silent flakes.

The snow soon stopped and for the rest of the day sunlight seeped through the whitened sky and thawed us out. But when we got the cattle as far as the meadow on lower Beaver Creek, still a good distance from our destination, the warmth declined behind the mountains and our breath froze in midair.

We left the herd for the night and rode at a trot to the swinging bridge and made our way across. As we turned upriver, with two and a half miles to go, darkness was overtaking the light. To save time, we soon turned our horses off the road to stay low along the river. But the breeze coming off the water was bitter and strong and caused our eyes to fill. We kept on a steady, hurried trot through the grassy bottom.

My cheeks stung and my lips felt fat and stiff. The constant jarring from my horse gave me a side ache and kept my pants working as sandpaper on the inside of my legs. Hunched forward and standing in the stirrups, I felt myself growing weak.

Suddenly, the river hurled its dampened frost in my face as if to say that it wasn't going to let up, so unless I wanted to give up and just fall off, I'd better toughen up. Determined to be hardy like Nonie and Bobby, I felt a surge of strength straighten my spine. I lifted my eyes and met the deepening cold head-on.

Dad turned in his saddle to look at me. Without slowing down, he jerked off one of his gloves and handed it to me.

"Here you go. Hold this over your face."

Dad's concern gave me more grit. Concentrating on the rhythm of the horse beneath me, I squinted my eyes behind the big glove, held tightly to the reins with my other hand, and rode for home.

It was dark when we got to the tack shed. "I'll turn the horses loose," Dad said. "You kids get to the house."

Walking on cold and tender lumps for feet, the three of us hurried up the path. When we pulled on the porch screen door, Mom opened the kitchen door, releasing a rush of toasted light soaked with aromas of frying and baking. Suddenly her grin disappeared and she grabbed me with both hands, saying, "Gosh-o-ziggity, girl!"

After rushing me into the kitchen, she quickly laid her hand across my cheek and began gently massaging. Before long the white patch regained its circulation. Then Mom directed us to slowly put our hands into an enamel washbasin holding a small amount of barely warm water. Needles shot through our red fingers, causing tears to trickle down our cheeks. Cooing to us, she ever so gradually warmed the water by pouring in small amounts of hot water from the teakettle. Finally the throbbing subsided.

Cold breezes were forgotten as we scooted our chairs up to the supper table. A large platter of breaded deer chops steamed alongside a jar of homemade chili sauce that smelled of cinnamon and cloves. Pulling apart hot biscuits, we lathered them with a mixture of butter and honey. Then we filled our plates with the fried chops, mashed potatoes and cream gravy, sweet hunks of baked hubbard squash, and cabbage slaw. When our plates were empty, Mom cut an applesauce cake filled with raisins and walnuts into squares.

Then she spooned thick, warm vanilla sauce over the top of each one before handing them out.

After the dishes were done, Dad laughed while telling us riddles and tongue twisters then sang to us of a strawberry roan and how the frog went a-courtin'. When he pulled me on his lap and jiggled his knee in rhythm with the songs, the tally book in his shirt pocket ground uncomfortably into the side of my face and the stubble on his chin scraped and reddened my forehead. Could there be a more wonderful throne for a kid?

On cloud nine I was sleepy and warm with my belly full. And I'd finished the day's work with my head up, while I rode stirrup to stirrup with Nonie and Bobby and this hardened and tender man, our dad.

Below: *Flooding river ice in an ice jam at Bridgeport, Utah, in about 1909.*
Bottom: *Upper Brown's Park near the John Jarvie Ranch.*

Top: *Nell Jarvie, wife of John Jarvie, about 1880.*
Left: *John Jarvie of Brown's Park in the late 1800s.*

*Bill, taking a thresher across the old
swinging bridge in the 1940s.*

CHAPEL OF WINTER BLUE

While passing around hamburgers and malts from a little cafe in Rock Springs called Riley's, we headed south on Highway 430 in our Ford sedan. It had snowed most of the day. Now that it was almost dark, the clouds were clearing away. When we finished the burgers, tasty with onion and mustard, we wadded up greasy bags and looked into the crystal night. Breaking trail as we went, we watched our headlights and the moonlight drip sparkles across the mounds and valleys of snow.

"These roads are slicker'n Toby's hinder," Mom said. "Sing to me, kids."

None of us thought to ask who Toby was, but we all began to sing. It eased the tension as she knew it would. This was a routine trip that would take us from Wyoming into Colorado and then into Utah, so we could have the privilege of spending Christmas vacation on the outskirts of Heaven.

Fifty miles later the pavement ended. We hadn't seen any other travelers, and with fifty miles of dirt road to go, we didn't expect to see any. Except where it happened naturally, the dirt roads were not even graveled. During trips like these when we were bucking snow, Mom sometimes had to make three or four runs at certain hills before the car could claw its way over the top. Sometimes we got out and pushed; other times the boys shoveled and laid sagebrush branches under the tires for traction.

A short while after crossing the Colorado state line, we passed near the Buckley and Dickinson Ranches. Daughters of a prominent cattleman, Charles Sparks, Margaret married Wright Dickinson and

Martha married Kenneth Buckley. Continuing the Sparks operation, the two families ranched side by side and were considered part
of the Brown's Park community.

Then we made our way into Irish Canyon. The long canyon
had served as a main route to Brown's Park since the early days for
mountain men, stockmen, prospectors, homesteaders, and outlaws.
Somewhere among its evergreens and boulders coated with snow, a
treasure was supposed to be hidden. Long ago some Irishmen
robbed a saloon in Rock Springs and high-tailed it south. They
were reported to have stashed part or all their loot in the canyon.
Because of the incident, Irish Canyon got its name and many folks
gained an elusive treasure to seek. It was fun to search the nooks
and crannies with our eyes and imagine becoming rich.

♣

Once when we were traveling from the ranch back to Rock
Springs in a blizzard, our car stalled in Irish Canyon. Mom wasted
no time with indecision. Immediately she bundled up and hurried
to gather wood for a fire and some hefty rocks to heat.

"We'll be fine," she promised. "We'll wrap the hot rocks in the
car blankets and put them on the floorboards, and they'll keep our
feet warm for hours. That's how we traveled in wagons in the winter when I was a kid. And you know we've got a big pan of fresh
cinnamon rolls and a couple gallons of milk in the trunk. We'll just
let the wind whistle and live it up till somebody comes along."

Not long after, someone did come by and got the car running. As
we drove away, heading to Rock Springs, I felt a little disappointed
that we never got the opportunity to fish those rocks from the fire.

♣

Just after leaving the mouth of Irish Canyon on our way to the
ranch for Christmas, we passed the turnoff to Reg and Floy
Buffham's place. A short distance later we turned off the main road
onto a narrower one.

"Look out there and just imagine," Mom said. "It was about
this same time of year and probably this much snow on the ground
back in 1898, when right along in here a Brown's Park posse chased
outlaws Harry Tracy, Dave Lant, and Pat Johnson. Johnson had
shot and killed a teenager named Willie Strang at the Red Creek

Ranch just northeast of Brown's Park before joining up with Tracy and Lant who had just escaped from the Utah pen."

Mom loved the history of our valley and we loved listening to the stories. Continuing she said, "As the posse was tracking the men up the side of that mountain over there, they had to lead their horses through the deep snow. But when they got too close, Harry Tracy shot and killed the posse leader, Valentine Hoy. Hoy owned the Red Creek Ranch where the whole thing started," she explained.

"Anyway, the posse had to give up and come off the mountain well after dark. But they ended up finding John Bennett, another one of the outlaws, at his camp right over there, near the mouth of Lodore Canyon. They lynched him down here at the Bassett Ranch." She shook her head. "It took fifty or sixty lawmen from Utah, Colorado, and Wyoming to chase those other three down. Those birds went many miles on foot with no supplies and wound up plumb over by Powder Wash before they got caught. Their feet were raw and bloody and they kept from starving by killing a colt to eat. All those lawmen from different states working together for the first time was the beginning of the end of the outlaws running loose in this part of the country."

We drove by the road leading to the first ranch in Bull Canyon on the east edge of Brown's Park. The Hoy family named the canyon in the 1800s when they wintered herds of bulls there. Favored with the heat of warm underground springs and fertile soil, fruit trees, peanuts, wildlife, and all sorts of other life flourished within the steep rock walls. Bob and Dorothy Simpson, a kind and happy young couple, purchased the ranch in 1952 from Della Worley, mother to one of Mom's closest childhood friends. The Simpson kids were our good friends.

Finally the valley of Brown's Park opened before us as a sleeping beauty dressed in moonlit blue and white. The air was noticeably warmer. Many of the ridges and hillsides were bare of snow, providing access to food for livestock and wildlife.

We saw the remains of the old Bassett Ranch where the lynching of John Bennett took place and where Ann Bassett, Queen of the Cattle Rustlers, was raised. Mom reminded us that Grandma and Grandpa Taylor first met Queen Ann when they were traveling to Brown's Park in their covered wagon, and remained friends with her. Sometimes Grandma would wrap up some goodies, which always included a couple of freshly baked coffee cakes, and load them and the kids into the horse-drawn wagon and drive the thirty or so miles to visit Ann for a couple of days.

There was a kinship between Mom and Queen Ann in the fierce way they loved Brown's Park and the old time cowboy way of life. Mom could easily have been describing herself when she expressed how Queen Ann could ride and rope. Although there was certainly a rougher edge to Queen Ann and some of her methods, Mom deeply understood why Ann battled against the huge Two-Bar outfit during the range wars in the 1890s and early 1900s, when floods of cattle kept encroaching on Brown's Park's grazing area. I knew if Mom had been born a little earlier and had been given the chance, she would gladly have ridden beside her when, armed and steadfast, Queen Ann patrolled the range.

"I was sorry to hear that Queen Ann had a heart attack at her home in Leeds, Utah, a couple of years ago," Mom said. "From what I understand she hasn't been able to regain her strength. She sure has led a colorful life. She knew Butch Cassidy and other members of the Wild Bunch very well, and she always considered them her friends."

Queen Ann would pass away the next spring, on May 9, 1956. Queen Ann's husband would then fulfill her last request by placing the urn containing her ashes in the Bassett cemetery so the Brown's Park winds could return her to the rocks, sagebrush, and cedars of her valley.

We then drove by the Blevins Ranch where Tom and his wife, Freddie, raised cattle. About twelve ranches were located in pretty spots throughout the valley. Most dated back to the beginning of the cattle herds in Brown's Park and had their individual stories to tell. The community also included several other ranch families who lived beyond Brown's Park's borders. The community was content and comfortable with its way of life, even though it was without such luxuries as telephones or electricity.

This was a hard-working and social community where the people gathered often. Dances at the Lodore School Hall, which was heated in the winter by a potbellied stove, brought people from near and far and lasted until dawn. Meetings of the women's organization of which Mom was a charter member, the Brown's Hole Home Demonstration Club, brought entire families together for potluck meals on a regular basis with some traveling forty or more miles to join in. Summer meant a Fourth of July picnic on Little Mountain or Cold Spring Mountain, and winter brought card-playing parties and holiday celebrations. We also attended weddings, funerals, and barbecues.

For every social occasion we each spiffed up, bathing in a metal washtub with water heated on the stove. The men wouldn't think of not shaving or polishing their boots and were certain to wear their good shirts and hats. Although ranchers made up the majority, in the mix would likely be a prospector, a government trapper, a road worker or two, and a couple of game wardens. The ranch women were superb cooks and the food was always plentiful.

⚭

When our car topped the hill overlooking the swinging bridge crossing the Green River, we were suddenly face-to-face with the range of our ranch. My memory of this view of Diamond Mountain never quite prepared me for the beautiful way it held up the sky. Its deep blue, cloaked with pearly drifts of deep snow, told us in a warm voice that we were home.

We were thankful to have this brand new swinging bridge to cross. The old swinging bridge had no side rails, simply having planks laid side by side and bolted on their edges to a cable frame. It was once described in the *Salt Lake Tribune* as "a ring-tailed doozie." Sitting high above the water, the bridge was narrow— only a little more than nine feet wide. However, it stretched from bank to bank for a distance of 304 feet, making for a long trip for travelers holding their breath.

Although I was just a baby when it happened, much too young to remember, I heard the story many times:

It was raining and blowing that Friday and well after dark when Mom stopped the car at the edge of the old bridge. Stuffed into the car were most of us kids, Mom, and a family friend, Luella Logan. Luella was already feeling a little anxious about traveling at night in such bad weather. But the young woman began to shake when the car's headlights landed on the bridge. They instantly revealed that the bridge was not only pitching to and fro but also heaving and bucking up and down.

Mom reached over and gave Luella a reassuring pat on the arm. "Now everybody be real still," she said. Then Mom slipped the car in gear, slowly let out the clutch, and steered onto the bridge.

As it always did, the weight of the car caused the bridge to hump up and moan as the car moved forward. Suddenly Mom took her foot off the gas and brought the car to an abrupt halt. Everyone stared ahead with big eyes at a gaping hole in the bridge. Mom kept her voice calm. "Looks like the wind has blown some of the boards off. Everyone just stay here. I'll get out and see what I can do about it."

The car was bobbing like a cork in a pond when Mom opened the door. When she climbed out, the strong wind whipped her hair and coat as it pelted her with rain. She got down on her hands and knees in the narrow space beside the car and crawled to the rear. In the red light of the taillights, she pulled and yanked until she got three planks to come loose. Dragging the planks as she went, she crawled to the hole in front of the car and laid them across it. Then Mom crawled back to the car and climbed inside.

"This is going to work just fine," she panted.

She started the car moving. Then, over the patched hole and across the bridge we went. Finally, the tires bumped off the end of the bridge and gripped solid ground.

As Luella released her terror with giggles and tears, Mom and us kids joined in with our own laughter. In the midst of everyone's relief, Mom took just a moment to feel the weakness in her legs. Then she took a deep breath, smiled, and drove on.

Not long after, the bridge broke apart and came down. For about the next four years we crossed the river at the mouth of Swallow Canyon in a rowboat or we walked across it on the ice. Each Friday night Dad watched for our car lights to blink over the top of the hill on the other side of the river; then he hurried to his pickup to come and get us. As we drove down the steep hill to the river, Dad's headlights always met ours. Leaving our car on the north side of the river, we crossed by foot or boat, then piled into the pickup and rode to the house. We made all our trips this way until the new bridge was finished on July 23, 1954.

Soon after crossing the new bridge, we passed from Colorado into Utah while enjoying the sight of several bunches of deer and a couple of jackrabbits. Arriving home we hurried down the pathway to the house and were happy to find Dad had a large chunk of coal burning cherry-red in the belly of the stove in the living room, which was chasing the chill from the bedrooms.

First thing after breakfast the next morning, we went for a short drive in Dad's pickup to find a Christmas tree. Before long the pine, lush with fragrance, stood decorated with shiny bulbs, ropes, and figurines. Nonie, Bobby, and I celebrated by scooping some fresh snow and mixing it with plenty of vanilla, sugar, and cream to make snow cream. We couldn't resist adding some of Mom's food coloring and laughed when our tongues turned green.

After dark the family drove around the bend of the rocky hill to the frozen lakes and built a bonfire to roast marshmallows and warm up. We sailed across the ice until the toes of our skates hit air holes where tules were sticking up, causing us to take one header after another. It didn't take long before we decided it was a lot more fun to get rid of the skates and slide around on the leather soles of our cowboy boots.

Santa arrived on Christmas Eve after it was announced that he had landed his sleigh in the corral. We were told, "He lands there so his reindeer can eat hay from the manger." We knew the score, but it was exciting just the same.

When Santa burst through the door in his red suit and fluffy beard packing a gunnysack filled with presents, we laughed and clapped. I did my best to ignore that Santa looked an awful lot like our brother Charlie, who was supposed to be busy elsewhere. And it truly was a temptation to say, "Excuse me, Santa, is that tape holding on your eyebrow?" Instead I giggled when he handed me a chubby doll in a bride's dress and then a colorful Indian headdress and matching bow and arrows. Tipped with little rubber suction cups, the arrows were just right for licking and sticking on Nonie and Bobby's foreheads.

As the celebration continued, we played our new board games and popped popcorn. And, as always on Christmas Eve, we pulled hot taffy until it cooled to glistening ribbons of sweetness.

"Better call Arlie, I guess," Mom said. "I can't find the taffy recipe."

We had a single phone line that extended only across the river to the Willow Creek Ranch where the Steve and Arlie Radosevich family had lived since 1932. Mom and Arlie had known each other since they were children. Arlie was born in Brown's Park at the Spitzie place and was the daughter of Charlie and Amelia Teters. Charlie Teters was at the Red Creek Ranch the day Willie Strang was shot. Years later a son whom Charlie and Amelia named after Valentine Hoy died at Red Creek of spinal meningitis and was buried beside Willie Strang.

Arlie's husband, Steve, was a game warden and rancher. Sometime during the holidays we were sure to spend an evening at their ranch enjoying all kinds of treats while hearing songs flow from their player piano.

As soon as Mom got the taffy recipe from Arlie, the candy making began. Before long we each had a large buttery piece of brown taffy, pulling, twisting, and yanking for all we were worth. Nonie, Bobby, and I gave up before long because we couldn't resist eating it, but Mom worked her taffy until it turned a pretty blonde shade.

Early the next morning, Mom filled a freshly plucked turkey with the sage-seasoned stuffing she had stirred together in her huge bread-mixing pan. Then she placed the turkey in one of the ovens to roast. The house filled with family and guests. The pantry was stacked with desserts, most of which Mom had spent the last couple of days making. There were pecan, coconut cream, pumpkin, lemon meringue, and buttermilk raisin pies. Also fruitcake, black walnut million dollar fudge, and creamy peanut butter fudge crowded among the pies.

While the guys gathered in the living room to visit, all the females, young and old, became part of a busy kitchen. Mounds of peels formed as a couple of the women prepared the white potatoes for a pot of boiling water. Mom layered sliced sweet potatoes, brown sugar, and butter into a baking pan. Someone else stirred the cranberries as the red gems danced in simmering sugar water. Lucille grabbed a pan of orange gelatin from the fridge and folded in some whipped cream and home canned apricots before adding a cheese topping to what was just one of three different gelatin salads. Mom handed Nonie and me a bowl of freshly blanched almonds and asked us to peel off the skins so she could add the nuts to the pineapple salad. "And then, girls," she said, "count heads so we can get the table set."

Just after Mom removed the heavy roasting pan holding the turkey and stuffing from the oven, she replaced it with her freshly risen yeast buns. Warm aromas had long since filled the house and even seeped outside. But the baking bread compounded the deliciousness in the air.

Mom put a lump of butter, some cream, and plenty of salt and pepper into the cooked and drained white potatoes; then Nonie and I took turns using the potato masher until the lumps were gone. We plopped the steaming creaminess into a bowl and added another bit of butter and a sprinkling of paprika on top. By then Mom had thickened the rich gravy she made from turkey drippings, seasoned both the corn and peas with pearl onions, and carved the turkey. Just moments before the meal was served and with perfect timing, she opened both oven doors and removed the candied, marshmallow-topped sweet potatoes and two large pans of golden buns.

As we sat down, in mid-afternoon, to enjoy the many bowls and platters of food, we grew quiet as the blessing was said. Mountain steeples surrounded us, and winter birds sang in the choir. We knew exactly whom to thank for the delicate ice lace and pretty winter-reddened willows along the creeks and for all the food before us.

Later on, when Mom saw we were tiring of indoor work and games, she smiled and said, "You three twerps bundle up and get outside and let the stink blow off."

Nonie, Bobby, and I ran toward the corral. Jumping on an old buckboard, we pretended to whip our twenty-mule team with baling twine tied on sticks and hollered the way we figured mule skinners would sound.

Before long we were in the corral, and I was bellowing and bucking in the wooden chute. As I was just the right size, I was the calf. Nonie and Bobby did the job of branding, dehorning, and earmarking me with a curved stick.

Next we were bronc riders on fierce, make-believe horses. Suddenly Nonie, pretending to be Wild Bill Hickock, came out of the chute on a mean-eyed bronc. She grunted and squalled and bucked wildly across the corral. Twisting and jumping, she tumbled through the air and sprawled out on the snow. Bobby and I ran to her side.

Bobby shook his head. "That bronc got the best of him. Ole Wild Bill's dead."

Immersed in the role, I began to cry. The whole thing was too real with Nonie lying there so still with her eyes closed. And once I got started bawling, it took pats and hugs from both Nonie and Bobby to convince me there was no reason to have my heart broken.

Feeling the cold and realizing it was getting dark, we started walking to the house. A lone star twinkled above the mountain, and I sadly squeezed my eyes closed and wished on the star that Nonie and Bobby would always be safe.

After going inside, we kept time to the music as Charlie and Les played their guitars and sang one song after another. Then, with tired eyes, Nonie and I headed to bed. After cupping her hand around the top of the lamp chimney, Nonie blew out the small flame. As we climbed under the covers on the brass bed, our feet were still cold from our time outside.

"If you let me put my feet on you till they're warm, then I'll let you put yours on me," Nonie said.

My teeth chattered when her feet pushed against my shins. Mom had done the best she could for us: the sheets were flannel; the mattress was stuffed with feathers; and there were so many layers of wool blankets, I'm surprised we ever walked right.

Once she warmed up, Nonie moved her feet away. As I started pushing mine toward her, she grumbled, "Try it and I'll slug ya." That was the privilege of being the older sister.

A couple minutes later I was listening to the low hooting of a great horned owl when Nonie softened. "Well, okay," she said. "You can put your feet over here, but just for a *little* while."

There we were, two country girls snug in our bed with our bodies and spirits well nourished. Outside, frozen moonlight clung to bare branches and lit the way for deer to tiptoe through the snow and find things to nibble. The beams melted as they streamed through the windowpanes and spread a layer of cream across our bedroom. Then we slept, as our Christmas home stood in a distant valley tucked within the mountains of Heaven-painted winter blue.

Top: *King's Point at Swallow Canyon on the Brown's Park Livestock Ranch.*
Above: *Nonie, Bobby, Diana, and Les Allen playing in the snow at the ranch.*

Opposite top: *Bill and Marie load the car in preparation for the family's return to Rock Springs.*
Opposite bottom: *The swinging bridge in 2005.*

Jesse Taylor at about 20 years of age.

I'LL THROW YOU A BISCUIT!

Perched on a slope covered with quaking aspen, sage, and pine, our one-room mountain cabin stood at the head of Galloway Draw in Colorado. Located just over a ridge from the Three Corners marker designating where Colorado, Utah, and Wyoming touch, the log cabin sat in the heart of our cattle's summer range.

Sitting on the bed, Nonie, Bobby, and I watched Mom throw the last of the dishwater onto the bushes outside and hang a flour sack dishtowel on a nail. Purple and yellow wildflowers drank spring water in a jelly jar vase placed in the center of the table, and a teakettle whispered a simmering tune from its spot on the wood cookstove.

Dad built this cabin alone in 1936 as he recovered from the ether pneumonia he contracted at Mom's side during the birth of their first child. We came here several times each summer, and our cowboys stayed here off and on when working cattle or fixing fence. This morning our older brothers and hired men met up with our cousin Allen Taylor. Watching the cowhands ride through the trees handling their lariats made us three kids itch to go along. But it wasn't yet our time to do the heavy riding.

Nonie led as we ran out the door. As we followed a cow trail, we listened to squirrels scold us from the tops of pines and smelled a sweet and spicy blend as we climbed to the top of a ridge. From there we could see far into the distance as mountains and valleys lifted and dropped away in hazy shades of pink, green, and blue. Dashing back down the steep trail, we splashed across the shallow creek at the bottom. Grabbing some strands of horse mane caught on a corral post, we hurried back to the spring-fed brook. We placed the coarse hair in the water and watched the black strands begin to wiggle as they seemed to come alive as hair snakes.

Later we tried to catch chipmunks in a coffee can. Then we fished in a beaver pond. It was bliss.

When it was time to get in the pickup and head home, Nonie, Bobby, and I climbed in the back, and we made our way slowly off the mountain. The trail-like road had Dad's truck nearly on its nose when Mom interrupted our singing. Pointing she said, "Look over there, you kids. There's a bunch of sage chickens." We turned to look. There were so many of the gray birds that the entire sagebrush slope seemed to be in motion.

Soon after turning onto the main road at the Myers Ranch, we started down steep Jesse Ewing Canyon. Before long we could see Jesse Ewing's old log cabin that was built in the 1800s.

Jesse Ewing was a stage station keeper on the Overland Trail and a miner at South Pass in Wyoming before he was a prospector here. John Jarvie told Grandpa Taylor that Ewing was a quiet, slow-talking man who never laughed out loud or wore any kind of coat in the winter. Although Ewing was small, he was wiry and tough-looking and no one who knew him had any interest in provoking him. The man seldom carried a gun but was never without a knife.

When Ewing built his cabin, he also dug a mine into a nearby hillside. He stayed to himself a lot of the time. It was a bit of a surprise to John Jarvie when Ewing returned from a trip to Green River, Wyoming, with a red-haired woman named Madame Forrestal and moved her into his cabin. No one saw much of the woman.

One midwinter afternoon, Jesse Ewing met up with a few other men at an abandoned military outpost across and up the river from the Jarvie store. A rock building there had been converted into a saloon, and the group of men gathered this day to play poker and drink whiskey. Among the card players sat a young cowboy and newcomer to the area named Charlie Roberts.

Many hours later when Charlie Roberts quit the game and walked out into the cold night, his pockets were heavy with his winnings, mostly from Jesse Ewing.

After stepping off of the bank, Roberts began crossing the frozen river. Suddenly, something hit him in the back and the young man sprawled face first into the thin layer of snow on the ice.

The next morning, the Jarvies were preparing for the day when Jesse Ewing opened the store door, stuck his head inside, and said, "Go on up the river a ways, Jarvie, and you'll find the prettiest corpse you ever saw." Then Ewing shut the door and headed back in the direction of his cabin and woman. John Jarvie put on his coat and hurried up the river where he soon saw a crumpled form lying on the ice.

"My goodness, the tracks in the snow were plain," John Jarvie said. "Ewing had to have jumped a good fifteen feet to stab that boy. Don't know how he did it, but the tracks were there."

No one knew the Roberts boy very well or where he was from. He was buried next to the saloon in as deep a grave as the Brown's Park men could dig in the frozen ground. The men finished the burial by piling river rocks over the dirt mound. Although the law from Vernal conducted a brief investigation, Ewing pled self-defense and the case was not pursued. There was very seldom any law presence in Brown's Park at that time, so this outcome was typical for such events.

Not long after the killing of Charlie Roberts, a husky man by the name of Duncan showed up at the Ewing cabin looking for work. Ewing offered Duncan a job working with him in the mine, and the pay included room and board.

There is no way to know how the plan between Madame Forrestal and Duncan was formed. But the redhead probably saw Duncan as her best chance to get far away from the life she was living. A couple of weeks after Duncan arrived, Ewing was ambushed in the cedars near his cabin, shot twice with a rifle, and killed.

A short time later, Duncan and Madame Forrestal stopped their horses at the Jarvie store. They told Jarvie that Ewing was sick back at the cabin and needed help. Then the pair quickly rode away, taking with them everything they could pack of Ewing's valuables.

No word of Madame Forrestal ever came back to Brown's Park. But Duncan, the man who freed her from Ewing's grip, eventually showed up in southern Utah, where he took his own life.

When Mom was a young girl and rode near the crumbling rock saloon on the old military road, she felt deep sorrow for the young cowboy who was killed by Jesse Ewing. Several times she picked bouquets of wildflowers for him. Frightened but determined, she said she usually rode very slowly to Charlie Roberts' grave. Once there she jumped off her horse, quickly placed the flowers on the rock-covered grave, then got back on her horse and hurried away.

⁂

A few minutes later we were out of the canyon and following an old fence of cedar post and barbed wire on Uncle Jesse's ranch. Here, just across the river from Grandpa Taylor's ranch, Uncle Jesse and his schoolteacher wife, Mattie, raised Mary, Claude, Allen, Roy, and Orville.

Uncle Jesse, tall and handsome, did most of his cowboying on a big, rawboned white horse with reddish freckles. To his children, their dad was never more handsome than the day he brought in a herd of wild horses off Mountain Home with neighboring cowboys Sam Carr, Frank Myers, and Walt Myers. The Taylor kids felt privileged to get to stand in the doorway of their school at Bridgeport and watch the cowboys and colorful horses race by on their way to their dad's corrals. The kids thought Uncle Jesse looked magnificent as he stood high in the stirrups, waved his hat, and sailed along on the impressive white gelding behind the rushing herd. It was a brief event that became a cherished memory for the youngsters.

The Taylor kids grew to be good hands. Each was attractive with a quiet, polite personality. Considered the ringleader by her brothers, Mary led them along cattle trails on bobtailed horses. Sometimes she rode a handy red roan with a bald face. Because the horse attracted ticks, Allen teased his sister by nicknaming the horse "Old Tick Bite." But Mary's favorite horse was a little red dun named Buck. With her long, slender legs and straight posture, Mary was impressive on the back of any horse.

Nonie, Bobby, and I admired their home. Created from Charlie Crouse's buildings moved from Bridgeport, it was wonderfully rustic. The two-story log home had a nice front porch, a wood cookstove in the kitchen, and a steer head hanging in the living room. A nick in one horn from a bullet was a reminder of the time the red and white steer nearly killed Grandpa Taylor.

The steer had belonged to the Sevens outfit east of Brown's Park near Craig, Colorado. Several times the Sevens cowboys tried to drive the steer home, but he always slipped away in the night, returning to Cold Spring Mountain to join with Grandpa's herd.

One fall a representative from the Sevens Ranch told Grandpa if he would bring the steer in when he gathered the rest of his herd and butcher him, he could keep the hide, head, and half the meat.

It was late fall when Grandpa and Uncle Jesse, then a young man, gathered and brought the herd off the mountain. The steer was eight years old, weighed around sixteen hundred pounds, and was as tall as a saddle horse. Nearing the house, the steer balked and refused to stay with the others and cross the river on the ice.

With the sun getting low in the sky, Grandpa said, "There's no sense fighting him. We'll go over to the house and get things ready and just butcher him here."

An hour or so later, carrying a meat saw, rifle, and two butcher knives, Grandpa and Uncle Jesse walked in the direction of the steer. Feeding in the sand knolls near the river, the steer kept jerking his head up and watching Grandpa and Uncle Jesse as they got closer. Uncle Jesse grew uneasy.

"That thing looks like he's gonna take after us."

Grandpa nodded. "Let him come."

Figuring they were close enough, Grandpa raised the rifle and fired. But the bullet missed the intended spot between the steer's eyes and hit low in the bridge of his nose. Blood trickled from the wound as the steer shook his massive head. Then he blew hard through his nostrils and charged.

Uncle Jesse spun around to run just as he heard Grandpa yell, "Don't run! You can't outrun him!"

Turning back he saw Grandpa struggling to get a jammed cartridge out of the rifle as the steer, carrying his horns low to the ground, was closing in with long lopes.

Just as the steer reached him, Grandpa dropped flat on his back. Horns swept across the top of Grandpa's body, stripping a glove from his hand and pitching it high into the air. Sailing over the top of Grandpa, the animal landed on the rifle, breaking the stock in two.

Bellowing, the steer turned and repeatedly jumped back and forth across Grandpa, bunting him with his head and trying to hook him. But because his horns curved upward, he couldn't find his mark.

Desperate to help, Uncle Jesse screamed and ran at the animal. He grabbed the steer's tail and pounded on his rump, but the steer ignored him. Sand was slung in every direction as the steer kept after Grandpa until exhaustion and the loss of blood began to weaken the animal. With eyes glazed, the steer fell to his knees.

Grandpa grabbed one of the steer's front legs and yelled, "Get him by the tail and maybe we can get him down."

Uncle Jesse couldn't budge the huge steer. Instead he grabbed Grandpa by the hand and pulled him free. The steer stayed on his knees as Grandpa and Uncle Jesse got away. Although they wished they could finish the steer off and not leave an injured animal, the rifle lay broken on the ground. Also, while Grandpa wasn't critically injured, he was seriously roughed up. Uncle Jesse's main concern was to get his father to the house so he could be looked after. Given the circumstances, including the lateness of the evening, taking care of the steer would have to wait.

The next morning the two rode horses when they went after the steer. Uncle Jesse's first shot glanced off the left horn, taking a nick from it. The next one slammed into the steer's neck and the battle was over.

Looking at the steer head hanging on Uncle Jesse's wall, I knew I wouldn't want to tangle with him. His black-tipped horns were sharp at the point and he still had a mean look in his eyes.

Just as Nonie, Bobby, and I wished we could work cattle with our cousin Allen and the others on the mountain, Allen told us he had longed to jump up from his school desk at the Bridgeport school and work cattle with Grandpa Taylor. He didn't have to imagine Grandpa's voice like we did; he actually heard the cracking report of Grandpa's bullwhip and the sound of his voice on the wind. Having Grandpa Taylor as a major influence in his young life, Allen was bound to be quite a guy.

Grandma and Grandpa had left their ranch to move to Rock Springs by the time Allen became a teenager, but they still owned it. Allen was fourteen and his brother Claude eighteen when during haying season they stayed across the river at Grandpa's ranch to do the haying there. Living in a small house Grandpa had built years ago for his mother, Nancy Taylor, Allen and Claude knew their dad was counting on them to finish putting up the second cutting of hay. What Uncle Jesse didn't know was that they were in possession of an ill-gotten shotgun.

A teacher at the Bridgeport School left one spring and decided not to return. Inside his living quarters, the teacher left behind a .410 shotgun and a box of #2 shells that were just up a notch from buckshot. The abandoned gun was irresistible to Allen and Claude. They slipped the gun out the door of the log building and kept it hidden.

Claude and Allen decided the gun wasn't quite western enough. They sawed off the barrel, took the stock off, and made a pistol grip. Claude fashioned a high, curled hammer resembling a flintlock. He amazed Allen the way he was so inventive and could figure out mechanisms.

Allen rubbed his hands together when Claude finished his work and said, "Boy, that looks better!" Then they hid the spare stock and barrel, figuring they'd make another gun before long.

After fashioning a holster from scraps of leather, the boys took turns packing the gun at the hip. "If a pheasant scares up and slaps me in the face, I'll just quick-draw," Allen said.

One morning they were working in the shop sharpening mowing sickles. They had a good share of the hay down, ready to stack. Allen had their nifty gun strapped on when Claude looked out the window.

"Look at those dang birds flocking into the cherry trees. Just when the cherries were gettin' ripe, too, and I had my mouth all set."

"Yeah, they can have the apples, but I don't want 'em eatin' up all the cherries from us," Allen said. He hurried toward the door. "I'll get 'em!"

The surprise explosion shattered through the building. Looking up, Allen saw dirt falling from the ceiling as he mumbled,

"What the heck?" Then he saw his gun lying across the room near the blacksmith forge with smoke curling from its barrel. Suddenly he grabbed his leg and ran out the door, loping around the grain drill twice before falling over. Holding his leg and howling, he watched blood soak his clothing and hands.

Claude hurried to pick Allen up. After he got Allen in the house, he said, "I think we'd better get something tied around that." Grabbing a couple of dishtowels, he pulled Allen's boot off. Blood poured from the boot and BBs rolled every direction.

"Oh, that's a terrible mess, Allen."

Wrapping the dishtowels around the wound, Claude shook his head.

"What are we gonna tell Pop? Maybe we can tell him a horse kicked you. You'll probably be limpin' for a day or two."

The dishtowels didn't do much good and the flow of blood continued. Growing fearful, Claude wrapped his brother in a blanket and gathered him in his arms. Although Claude was four years older, he wasn't much larger. Still, he carried his younger brother on the run across the meadow to the river. Claude left Allen lying in the willows while he hurried to get in Grandpa's old hand-over-hand trolley and pull himself across the river to get to the rowboat on the opposite bank. After Claude pushed the boat into the water, he jumped in and strained to move the oars against the current to hurry back to Allen.

Finally getting Allen in the boat and across the river, Claude packed him to the black 1928 Chevy coupe where it waited near the river in a shed. As they drove the mile or so to the house, they both knew they had to tell the truth and face their father together.

Uncle Jesse was concerned, but knowing his haying crew was shot in more ways than one, he was clearly very angry with both boys. The boys couldn't have felt worse as they drove away with their mother and headed to Rock Springs to a doctor.

Although there was talk of amputation by one physician, Dr. Roe told that pessimistic doctor to leave the room while sternly saying he would do whatever needed to be done. When Allen later awoke from the ether, he was terrified until he saw his toes poking up in the air.

Dr. Roe couldn't dig all the BBs out of the wound without causing more damage. "They'll work their own way out," the doctor said.

Arrangements were made for Allen to stay with our mom in Rock Springs, and she nursed him to a full recovery. He became a popular attraction in homeroom at school as his friends "operated" with a pocketknife each time a BB rose just under the skin.

Although the metal beads continued to surface now and then, they never interfered with his cowboying. Allen was the only one of the Taylor boys who didn't go into the military. Claude decided to make a career of the Navy; Roy took first place in the bronc riding during a military rodeo in Hawaii; Orville became a paratrooper in the 101st Airborne. Mary worked in Oregon for a while and then returned home to marry Bill Baker and raise a family not far from Brown's Park in Maybell, Colorado.

Allen married Francis Graham, a beautiful dark-haired cowgirl who was raised on a ranch northeast of Brown's Park. Although he found work away from the ranch, he often returned to help Uncle Jesse. Francis described her exceptionally handsome husband as a bit arrogant and vain. Then as her eyes filled with affection, she added, "And the most beautiful man on a bucking horse I've ever seen."

Riding a good-looking Colorado Saddlery saddle, Allen was partial to spurs with big rowels. Sometimes he wore batwing chaps and other times he wore the shorter chinks. He preferred a one-ear bridle and made sure he had a fancy silver bit to dress it up. A perfectionist like Grandpa Taylor, he wanted his clothing and every piece of gear to fit just right.

Allen felt privileged to ride with and hear stories from some of the area's best "deadly ole hands." Though they were tough and leathery, they were nearly all seasoned with gentleness, good humor, and raw ability. Although they turned most of their mounts into good saddle horses, spending so much time in the saddle in rough country on edgy broncs meant there was bound to be some trouble.

A local cowboy named Arthur Roberts had a high, squeaky voice and was nicknamed "Slick" because his head since childhood only sprouted a few patches of fuzz. He worked as a ranch hand for several different outfits, including ours. Arthur ordered a saddle from the Fred Mueller Saddle and Harness Company in Denver and referred to his new saddle as "Old Mueller."

Arthur saddled a snaky gelding one early morning but without having his favorite horse, Twelve Days, to act as snubbing partner, he wasn't sure he wanted to climb in the middle of the gelding. Arthur stalled, fussed, adjusted, and readjusted Old Mueller.

Finally Brown's Park rancher and top notch cowboy Harry Carr hollered, "Ohhh, just get on there, Arthur. If you don't come down by dinner, I'll throw you a biscuit!"

Arthur nodded, climbed on the horse, and turned the wide-eyed bronc toward their day's work.

Arthur was about sixty years old when Allen was riding with him in Galloway Draw pushing cattle along a trail on a high slope. Arthur was working for Dad and was riding a sorrel gelding with a white star on his forehead. Without warning, the gelding named Red did as he was prone to do and started bucking off the side of the mountain through the timber. Hearing the racket that sounded like a herd of elk crashing through the trees, Allen wasn't sure he'd ever see Arthur alive again and decided he'd better try to head him off.

Allen saw Red's tracks in the boggy black mud in a meadow along the creek as he hurried to catch up with Arthur. The depth of the tracks was evidence that Red was coming down hard on his front feet and most likely still bucking.

Staying on a trot, Allen followed the tracks in a huge circle and wound up back where he started—at the cattle herd. When Allen rode up to Arthur, he saw that Red had settled down, and Arthur was checking himself and his saddle.

"Well, Old Mueller stayed put," he squeaked.

Except for a little blood coming off his head, he seemed no worse for the experience. Allen ducked his head and grinned.

Our brother Charlie took Red for one of his horses. Charlie liked him because Red was beautiful and a good traveler, but the horse stayed unpredictable. Sometimes without warning he ducked his head between his front legs and bucked violently through the brush. Though Red was usually on his best behavior when moving cattle, Charlie did a lot of his work with Red in a running buck. Red often kicked. Standing still or moving at a walk, it wasn't unusual for him to kick at his own tail or reach up with a back hoof and hit Charlie's spur, ringing the rowel. Once when John Story was riding across the river behind Charlie and Red, the sorrel kicked and connected with John's knee. That injury later prevented John from passing his physical to become a paratrooper so he had to settle for the regular army.

Once when Charlie was riding Red, the gelding spooked and took off in a dead run. Charlie pulled hard on the reins but Red ran all the faster, heading straight toward a barbed wire fence. At the last second before hitting the fence, Charlie loosened the reins. Red jumped high, easily clearing the fence, but when he came down he hit so hard on his front feet and with his head down that Charlie and the saddle were both yanked forward.

When the wild episode was over, Charlie was on the ground. He was still sitting in the saddle with his feet in the stirrups and he still had a grip on the reins. At the other end of the reins stood Red.

The next weekend when we returned to the ranch from school, Red was gone.

"It was kinda tough to sell him, Charlie," Dad said. "But after what I've seen, I had to get rid of him before you got hurt." We all knew Dad was right. But we were going to miss that pretty red horse.

As for our almost-brother, John Story, even if it meant he had to head into a frost-filled fog with snow reaching the top of his horse's knees, he enjoyed climbing on a bronc to do a day's work. John did his best to make a saddle horse out of a gelding from our wild herd named Sox. Sox didn't care that John would soon graduate from the University of Wyoming and go on to be the prominent manager of the Parker Land and Livestock Ranches near Dubois, Wyoming. John didn't know that Sox was destined to become the famous rodeo bucking horse called Mud Springs.

Riding Sox against the wind along the top of a hill with neighbor Walt Myers, John pulled his hat down on his forehead. Just then a swirling gust lifted one leg of his chaps and slapped the leather against the gelding's neck. Sox made three fast jumps forward. Then as chaps flapped and dirt and rocks flipped into the wind, Sox got his head between his legs and hit his powerful bucking stride.

Walt loped his horse alongside and hollered, "You want me to pick him up?"

"Ohhh, no," John grunted. "Just stay out of the way. I'm-gettin'-him-rode." But just a few moments later John hit the ground.

Getting to his feet, the young cowboy dug dirt from his eyes and looked up at Walt. "This is a heck of a thing to ask, I guess, but was I spurrin' him?"

Leaning back in the saddle Walt laughed. "You bet you was spurrin' him. Even when your head was draggin' in the sagebrush, you was spurrin' him."

✂

Many men and women of this distinctive breed rode the ridges of our world. Cowhands who saddled up and rode out from mountain cabins to gather cattle in the morning mist. There was wisdom in the eyes and movement of the hard-working cow horses with sweat curling the hair on their necks and flanks. These images are portraits—of a time, a place, and us.

Left: *C.M. Taylor crossing the Green River in his trolley.*
Below: *John D. Story riding Sox at the Brown's Park Livestock Ranch about 1952.*

Opposite top: *Jesse Taylor, Francis Taylor with daughter Linda, Allen Taylor, and Orville Taylor at their ranch in 1951.*
Far left: *Charlie riding Red at the ranch.*
Left: *Allen Taylor as a teenager.*
Above: *The Allen cabin shown down the steep slope from the corral, at the head of Galloway Draw on Cold Spring Mountain.*

Nonie Allen and her horse Chocko.

OF GRACE AND POETRY

Letting her gaze linger on the horse herd in the corral in the spring of 1956, Nonie, then eleven years old, finally smiled and pointed to a gangly, chocolate-colored youngster. The older boys started to laugh. "What do you want that ugly thing for? He's homelier than a mud fence. Look at him, he's got mule ears." Humiliated for herself and the tender-eyed gelding, Nonie walked to the house in tears with me, at six years old, following close behind.

Patting Nonie's cheek, Mom told her, "That's okay, honey. I'll bet he's cute as a bug's ear. Just remember it's a long old road that doesn't have a turn in it. I've got a sneakin' feeling you made a good choice."

Signs that Chocko was going to be something special were beginning to emerge by the time he was ready for a saddle. Growing into those grand ears and tent pole legs, he was quick to learn. When Nonie was thirteen, Les started Chocko for her but rode him only a few times before he turned the young gelding over to Nonie to finish. Chocko was considered green broke when Nonie pulled herself onto his back the first time. Everyone watched from a distance when she gently nudged him with her heels. After the first few steps, the horse and the girl began to get acquainted and develop trust. For a long time Bobby and I played in the dirt and watched through the wire fence as Nonie walked Chocko up and down the pasture, stroking his neck every little while.

A few days later our good buddies from Rock Springs, Kaylou and Louie Muir, came for a visit. Bobby and Louie, looking like a matched pair with their light hair cropped short, took off for parts unknown. Nonie couldn't wait to show Kaylou her horse. Peeking through the corral poles, Kaylou whispered, "You guys are so lucky."

&

Tall like Nonie and the same age, Kaylou had the kindest heart of anyone we knew. Her brother, Louie, was my age. Sadly, Kaylou and Louie's mother died when they were very young. They lived with their grandparents and policeman father across the street from our house in Rock Springs. They had a history connected to Brown's Park, and our families had known each other a long time: Amanderville "Mandy" Tolliver Wiggins was Charlie Crouse's half-sister and Kaylou and Louie's great-aunt through marriage.

Kaylou and Louie helped Nonie, Bobby, and me get through some pretty tough times. When our beloved little dog Midget died one night in her sleep, they helped us carry her to a quiet place on a hillside above the house. The five of us cried as we buried her there. And when Nonie ran around the corner of the chicken coop and accidentally squashed a baby chick under her bare foot, they mourned with us at that funeral.

They were our buddies, even when we got them hurt. Several times we lined up on my horse Bollie's huge back only to come tumbling off, stacking up in a heap of bruised elbows and hips. Kaylou carried a scar above her eye after smacking her head on the ice flowing over the bank of a ditch where we'd gone to skate.

&

After Nonie told Kaylou all about Chocko, we caught three other horses to go for a ride. Chocko wasn't ready for that kind of riding, but Nonie didn't want to leave him behind, so she decided to let him follow.

We each got a thrill out of loping our horses along a narrow trail that went off a small hill, dipped through a thicket of willows, and went up a hill on the other side where the ground flattened into a patch of sweet corn. It was like riding a roller coaster on horseback. Several times Chocko loped behind us as we charged through the willows.

After deciding it would be our last trip since the sun was going down, we dashed through the willows and topped the hill. Suddenly a cloud of mosquitoes rushed us, and I was caught completely off guard when my horse spun and ran back down the trail. Although I was pulling on the reins as hard as I could, I couldn't stop the mare from plunging into the willows.

The collision was head-on. Chocko's forehead hit me in the chest and stomach, knocking me high out of the saddle. I ricocheted through the willows and landed hard.

The next thing I knew Nonie had my horse in tow and was making sure Chocko was okay and that I'd live. She was doing all this while swatting mosquitoes and doing her best to keep Kaylou from going bonkers. Off her horse, Kaylou was squalling with her mouth wide-open. Sucking in her breath, she inhaled the bugs and bawled louder. It was quite a scene: I was scraped up and crying, the horses were switching their tails and turning in circles, and Nonie was trying to get Kaylou to just close her mouth.

Nonie finally managed to gather us up and get us back on the horses so we could run away from the worst of the swarm. After turning Chocko and the other horses loose in the pasture, we hurried to the house to dab some rubbing alcohol on our itchy bumps—especially poor Kaylou. Her body, unaccustomed to being munched on by mosquitoes, had a collection of bites swelling into welts. Before long, we were "doctored up" and running out the door.

The big alfalfa field where we grew most of our hay was about a quarter of a mile away from the house and on top of a hill. The west end of the field began at the foot of Diamond Mountain and spread out along the large flat surface, or bench, of the hill. We always referred to the area as "the bench."

About halfway between the house and the bench, a barbed wire fence came off the steep hill to a gate that crossed the road. The fence then continued northward from the gate through a little field to Crouse Creek and beyond. Although we didn't usually keep the gate across the road closed, at different times throughout the year it was necessary to shut it to keep livestock on one side or the other.

Mom and Dad talked it over with county officials and decided that placing a cattle guard across the road to serve as both fence and gate would be a wonderful convenience. The cattle guard would deter horses, cattle, and sheep from crossing but would allow haying equipment, trucks, and other traffic to pass freely.

Nonie, Bobby, and I walked up the road one afternoon to watch as two happy and friendly men constructed the cattle guard. They had already dug a pit with shovels the full width of the road. The hole was about two and a half feet deep. It went from one edge of the road to the other and spanned about eight feet in length. The men worked with heavy boards and timbers, saws, hammers, nails, and bolts to build the structure from scratch.

A couple of days later the wooden cattle guard was finished. Sitting level with the grade of the road and on top of the pit, the cattle guard had parallel rows of ten-foot-long 2x4s placed on edge and spaced about eight inches apart, all the way across the pit. Some 2x12 board blocks gave added support from below. Several yards down the fence line and not far from the creek, a new wire and pole gate that was built for the passage of livestock stood wide open.

When Nonie thought it was time for Chocko to advance from being ridden with a simple hackamore to a bit, she slid it into his mouth. Chocko opened and closed his mouth as he explored the bit with his tongue but accepted the bit without a fuss. She rode him around for a few minutes and he seemed fine, so she decided to take him on a short ride to the top of the bench and back. It was a decision she would soon regret.

After crossing the bridge over the creek, the pair turned up the road. When Chocko started to trot, Nonie pulled gently on the reins. But instead of slowing, Chocko misunderstood and trotted faster. Worried but having no idea what was wrong, Nonie pulled hard on the reins. Chocko clamped down on the bit and started to a gallop.

Nonie glanced ahead and was startled. She'd forgotten about the new cattle guard, and she knew Chocko had never seen it. Frantically she began yanking on the right rein, trying to turn Chocko off the road and aim him for the open gate, but the horse understood none of it. Instead he bowed his muscular neck and raced faster.

Beneath this wild beauty of girl and horse, no doubt a breeze was stirred as dark hooves lifted and dropped in elegant, violent, repeated strides. Perhaps this soft, spinning hand of nature plucked the seeds of dandelions while muscles and nostrils strained. The tiny wind may then have set the searching seeds adrift on puffs of dust as the thunder above moved closer to its fate.

By the time the young gelding saw the cattle guard, it was too late for him to stop . And although at that instant Nonie loosened the reins, leaned forward, and urged him to jump, it was too late for Chocko to collect himself well enough to clear the eight-foot expanse. But he tried.

If the awkward jump had taken him just a few inches farther, Chocko's front feet would have landed on the other side of the cattle guard. Instead, both his front feet came down in the space between the last two boards. Nonie's mind was flashing with thoughts of us back at the house and the fear that everything for her and Chocko was ending when Chocko's body tipped sharply and he fell headfirst. Nonie was flung forward, out of the saddle. The moment she slammed into the hard-packed road, her world went black.

There's no telling how long Nonie was unconscious, and there is no way to know how Chocko got out of the cattle guard with no broken legs. When Nonie opened her eyes, Chocko was standing next to her, trembling. Getting to her feet, she saw that all his legs were badly skinned and bloody. Then she saw blood trickling from his left knee where a stick was poking out.

Whimpering how sorry she was for what she had done to him, Nonie gathered Chocko's reins and rubbed his forehead. He limped behind her as she led him slowly to the nearby creek. Talking to him all the while, she washed the blood away then took hold of the embedded stick and pulled it from his knee. Pitiful and battered, they walked slowly home. Both would soon be okay, having gained some wisdom and maturity the hard way.

Time passed and the swan in Chocko fully emerged. The brownish black gelding stood taller than all the other horses on the place. High-strung and powerful, he truly frightened Grandpa Christensen because of the way he acted when Nonie got on him in the mornings. But Mom understood the performance.

"Don't you worry, Papa," Mom told him. "He knows he's pretty and he just likes to show off. I've watched that girl a half a dozen times climb under his belly and sit and comb his legs while he stands there asleep. He likes her. And she knows how to handle him."

After saddling Chocko with Aunt Bessie's saddle, a gift from Mom, Nonie knew to be ready for the dance as soon as she settled her weight on his back. She laughed as Chocko reared and lunged, leaping into the air again and again. They were a magnificent pair: at thirteen Nonie was also a beauty with long dark hair matching the color of Chocko's mane. Poetic and graceful, their rhythm was fluid, the enormous leaps smooth, and the landings easy. Their connection was solid and unique.

One afternoon Nonie was riding Chocko along the side of the rocky hill just above the lakes. Deciding to get off to look closer at a rock she thought might be an arrowhead, she swung out of the saddle, but she landed awkwardly on the slope and lost her balance. As Nonie stumbled backward, her other boot hung up on the leather tapadera covering the stirrup. She hit the ground with the flat of her back, but her leg stretched in the air with her foot still caught. Serious injury or even death could have easily been the outcome if Chocko had spooked and run with her caught on the stirrup. Instead, Chocko stood still except to turn his head to look at her. Kicking loose from the stirrup with her other boot, Nonie struggled to her feet. Hugging the big gelding's neck, she patted him and told him over and over that she loved him.

We hadn't been riding more than five minutes the next spring when Nonie touched her hand to Chocko's neck. "Something must be wrong here," she said. "Chocko's wringing wet. Look, he's sweating so bad it's dripping on the ground."

By the time we got Chocko back to the house, water was running off him in rivulets, and his eyes looked hollow and dull.

"Bring him in the yard into the shade and let's get the saddle off him," Dad said. "Maybe it'll help if we wipe him down with some cool water from the creek."

Standing in the shade of a giant boxelder, Chocko's knees buckled and he went down. Nonie cried as she held his head in her lap and washed his face. His moans broke her heart as she begged him not to die. Then Chocko's eyes began to clear. He sat up. Getting to his feet, Chocko raised his head to look around. As suddenly as the attack came, it retreated.

"The only thing I can figure is green grass poisoning," Dad said. "I don't believe it was colic because he never did kick at his belly and act like he had a bellyache."

⧫

Chocko was fully recovered when Dad asked Nonie whether she thought the three of us could trail the cows and calves the six miles to the summer range across Willow Creek and up the steep climb of Birch Creek all by ourselves. The job would take all day. Proud and excited, we all nodded and said we knew we could do it. We could hardly wait for morning.

After an early breakfast, Mom handed us each a hotcake sandwich rolled in wax paper to take along for lunch. "I'm just not going to worry about you kids. I know you're big enough to handle this, and the cows know the way so they should trail pretty well. You just be awful careful when you come back across that darned river."

Dad helped us gather the herd from the pastures, and Mom was at the river by the time we got ready to take them across. It was a bit of a battle and it took a lot of hollering and riding up and down the bank before the lead cow finally took her calf into the water. A few more followed and soon the entire herd went.

"Okay, you kids, get going on across and keep them moving," Dad said. "You're on your own."

Mom blew us a kiss and hollered, "Bye sugar-doogers. Just keep 'em pointed in the right direction and they'll go."

Nudging our horses into the river, we did as we were taught: holding the saddle horn, we gave our experienced horses their heads so they could make their own way across; we took our feet out of the stirrups and bent our knees as much as we could to stay dry; and we didn't stare into the water because the flowing motion would make us dizzy.

With my feet tucked under my rump, I thought back to my first time riding across the river, which was also my first memory in life: I sat on a pillow across the saddle horn in front of Mom, and Bobby was on a pillow behind her. We were riding Montan, Mom's beautiful bay mare. Coming out of the river, Bollie jerked me back to the present when he shook his body, rattling my teeth. My knees were soaked but I knew it wouldn't take them long to dry.

We were feeling pretty important as we gathered the cattle from the willows and started up the steep, sandy hill. I had my switch ready to help Bollie stay in gear, and Nonie and Bobby cowboyed the stragglers on Chocko and Smokey. Soon the sun began to heat up and we all settled into a slower pace. When I got thirsty, Bobby told me to suck on a little rock. It helped, but I still wanted a drink.

Watching cottontails dart for their hidey-holes and blue birds fly from perch to perch, we trailed through cedars and across open sagebrush flats. The calves, with their auburn hair gleaming in the sun, worked hard to keep up. Mother cows turned to bawl and smell the calves until satisfied their babies were there. Talking and laughing, the three of us teased each other and stayed on the move.

Clouds, huge and black, slid over the sun, cooling the air. "Looks like we might get a gully washer," Bobby said. But we only got the edge of the thunderstorm that ranted and boomed along the mountain. Nearing the end of the shower, rays of sun opened the clouds as cactus blooms glistened in candy colors and the air smelled of sweet mint. Droplets from the clouds looked like lavender leaves falling to the earth.

At the creek at the base of the mountain, we stopped to let the herd drink and rest. Willow Creek hurried over rocks and passed by pussy willows growing along the bank. The cows drank and then sauntered out of the creek, allowing it to clear. We moved upstream to lie on our stomachs and drank our fill. As we relaxed in the shade, we unwrapped our sandwiches and each dined happily on a hotcake wrapped around a fried egg and whole dill pickle.

Riding our horses away from the cool creek, we hit a barrier of heat. The sun scorched the moisture in the air left behind by the rain, turning it sultry. The cows didn't want to leave the tall grass and shade of the trees to walk uphill. The three of us split up and worked to prod our section of the herd. We were rosy-faced and sweating when we finally met up and pushed the cattle into one bunch. Then we headed up the climb on an old and rocky road through the cedars. Birch Creek didn't come this far down, so we wouldn't see any water running until we made it to higher country.

The cedars and rocks inhaled the heat and held it there. Every little while calves broke away, forcing us to circle around them to bring them back. Cows began to pant as slobber strung from their mouths. Several of them took their calves and hurried off the road and tried to hide in the shade of the cedars. Lather worked its way from underneath the saddle blankets on our horses.

"Don't you think this is far enough?" I asked Nonie.

"Huh-uh," she answered. "We have a long way to go yet. We just gotta keep at it."

My sweaty temples throbbed and my rear ached from the hours in the saddle. I waited a long time. Then, through lips that felt blistered, I asked again, "Are you sure this ain't far enough?"

"No. Now listen. We gotta do what we were told. Dad said to take them clear through the gate and even a ways beyond that."

Step after step ground into the dirt and rocks. When the fence finally came into view, it stretched across where the road ended. Bobby trotted Smokey ahead to get the gate open, and we took the herd through.

Later, when I figured we must have gone far enough, Nonie mentioned we still had a ways to go. So, among huffs and puffs and grunts, we left the fence farther and farther behind. Finally, the heat began to disappear as we reached the long, late afternoon shadows within a grove of aspens. Birch Creek trickled over rocks and roots and formed small, silver pools.

All of a sudden Nonie turned in the saddle and grinned at Bobby and me. "I believe this is plenty far enough, you yahoos!"

We let out with a whoop and turned our horses around. In that instant I was on a brand new horse. I threw my switch away as Bollie headed down the trail in as fast a walk as his big feet could manage. Chocko bobbed his head and Smokey strained against the reins. The cows would now spread out and graze their way up the final climb before reaching the top of the mountain. Our job was done and we were headed home.

Cast in black against the fading light, nighthawks darted overhead in the evening coolness. Riding three abreast, we laughed and relived the ups and downs of the day. We arrived at the river just after dark and frightened a great blue heron, which flapped its massive wings as it lifted out of the willows. Splashing into the river, Bobby followed Nonie and I followed him.

After our horses came out of the water, they broke into a trot. "My big-uns are eatin' my little-uns," Nonie giggled.

"Mine, too," Bobby said. "I wonder what Mom's got waitin' for us on the stove."

Proud and grinning, we strutted up the path after turning the horses loose. Mom and Dad met us at the door, anxious to hear about our day. We couldn't get it all told fast enough as we washed our hands and faces and sat down to a meal that included chili, rich with tomato and loaded with meat and plump beans; fresh leaves of garden lettuce stacked on a platter and drenched in a dressing made with cream, sugar, and vinegar; potatoes fried in bacon drippings; and large squares of warm corn bread.

A while later, Nonie sat back on the bench and leaned her head against the wall. "Whew!" she said. "I've ate so much I'm gonna bust."

Mom nodded her head and laughed. "Me, too. So pass the cornbread and crab apple jelly and get out of the way!"

When we went to bed that night, I couldn't keep from smiling. Mom and Dad had really bragged us up for getting that big job done all by ourselves. Closing my eyes, I trailed cows all the way to the top of the mountain and beyond.

About a week later the three of us ran into the kitchen from outside, carefree and laughing. The look on Dad's face brought us up short.

He looked at Nonie and said, "Do you know that when you took the cows up Birch you left a calf on this side of the fence? Well, he's dead."

She moved her head from side to side and uttered, "I-didn't-mean-to."

Turning around to stir sugar into his coffee, Dad ended with, "Well, there goes your winter shoes."

When Bobby and I caught up with Nonie, she was in the pasture with Chocko. Standing with her arms around his neck, she turned toward us as we walked up. She looked at us with sad, tear-filled eyes, and wiped her hand across her nose.

Bobby tilted his head and put his lips together in a half smile.

"It's okay, Non. Dad's not even mad. He told Mom that calf must have lain down and hid under a bush and he probably wouldn't have seen him either. He said that isn't much of a fence up there, and it shouldn't have stopped the calf's mother from coming back for him. Really, Non, he ain't mad."

"I know," she said softly. "It isn't about Dad so much. It was my job and I should have been more careful. I just can't stop thinking about that poor little thing lying up there and dying all by himself."

Then she leaned her forehead into Chocko's neck and sobbed.

⚭

With the gift of responsibility came the burden of accountability. The beautiful innocence of our childhood games on the Brown's Park Livestock Ranch was already fading. Try as we might we couldn't keep our lives still. We couldn't prevent Bollie and Smokey from getting too old and being culled from the herd and sold, any more than we could hold back the seasons that aged us.

Above: *Kaylou Muir, Nonie holding a duck, Diana, Louie Muir, and Bobby at the ranch.*
Right: *Bobby taking a friend, Louie Muir (in front), for a ride on Comet with Ring tagging along.*

Right: *Nonie at 14 years old.*

Below: *Louie Muir, Nonie, Kaylou Muir, and Diana riding Bollie.*

Diana's horse Spooks.

I HAD SPOOKS

Although Nonie, Bobby, and I still spent time together, our worlds often spun in different directions. Nonie and Bobby were in high school together, but I was still just shy of my teens. Nonie, with friends in Craig, Maybell, Vernal, and Rock Springs, was involved in rodeo queen contests and with rodeo cowboys. Bobby was often busy with guys and girls from school.

Watching my gelding's ears flick back and forth, I always talked to him when we made our way alone over the rocky hill heading to the sandy spot or some other place where memories lived. My town friends had diaries to cry into and tell of their growing pains; I had Spooks.

As the youngest in the family, I always ended up with horses no one else wanted. How lucky for me that no one had any use for this stocky, black-eyed palomino pinto with mane and tail the color of cream.

I knew the complaints: Spooks was a little clumsy; he spooked easily and often threw fits and broke bridles when left tied up; he once kicked the saddle out of Les's hands, then later the same day lost his footing and tumbled down a hill, breaking poor Les's big toe; and another day Spooks bowed his neck, took the bit in his mouth, and plowed through a dense thicket, leaving Charlie dangling on a clump of willows.

Even though Spooks did yank me around when he stumbled, and I broke a bone or two when I hit the dirt, I was willing to pay the price. He never kicked at me, he never broke my bridle, he was my gentle sweetheart.

One summer Mom and Dad agreed to let Bobby, his friend Jimmy Seppie, and me participate in the youth rodeo in Vernal. After hauling us and our horses over Diamond Mountain, Mom and Dad helped us get ready to ride in the parade and sign up to participate in some of the events at the rodeo grounds.

Waiting the first evening to go into the arena for the western pleasure class, I felt my excitement drift away as I began to feel embarrassed and out of place. The large group of contestants seemed sure of themselves, and their horses all were sleek with slim ankles and tiny feet. His coat was shiny enough, but there was nothing slim or tiny about Spooks.

Soon we were circling inside the arena, directed by the judge when to walk, trot, lope, stop, and reverse. My hat flew off the second time we galloped, but I ignored it as Spooks continued to do everything I asked of him. Finally it was over and we waited for the judge's decision. My heart pounded, but in the end I wasn't in the least surprised that we weren't in the small group of winners who were lined up and given ribbons and trophies.

As all the other riders left the arena, I turned Spooks around and rode him in a soft lope to where my hat was lying in the dirt. Sliding to the ground, I felt self-conscious in front of the stands filled with people. Pushing the hat down on my head, I suddenly realized the announcer's voice echoing through the loudspeaker was talking about me! I held my breath and hoped I wouldn't miss the stirrup as I grabbed the saddle horn with both hands and jumped the way Nonie and Bobby had taught me. When I felt my foot slide into the stirrup, I swung into the saddle.

"Ladies and Gents," the announcer was saying. "The judge and all of us up here in the booth were so impressed with this youngster and her rocking-chair-of-a-horse that the judge is creating a special award tonight. Young lady, you just stop by his western apparel store tomorrow and pick out any pair of jeans in the place, and they're yours."

Applause erupted from the crowd and I could barely believe my ears. Lifting my hand, I waved quickly then reached down to pat Spooks on his neck as we loped out of the arena and the limelight.

Through the years Spooks continued to do just about everything I asked of him, but we did have some bad wrecks. Taking a final ride with Barbara Francis, my best friend from Rock Springs who was moving with her family to Nebraska, we kicked our horses into a lope. Spooks was really picking up steam when he stubbed his hoof on a mound of dirt. In spite of fighting to keep his footing, he fell roughly to his knees, sending me rocketing headfirst into the bank of a hill.

Digging myself out of the dirt, I eventually found my way to my feet. Spooks was a little shaky but stood still as I climbed back on him to continue the ride. That night I felt awful because my best friend was gone and because of the bruises and strains left from smacking the hillside.

Each year after the first hard frost wilted the alfalfa, Dad put the bulls on the bench to graze. One fall day as I rode Spooks at a slow walk across the bench, two bulls started fighting. Spooks and I both watched the battle as the huge bulls bellowed and pawed the ground, throwing dirt into the air. They jammed their thick foreheads together and violently strained and pushed, knocking each other all over the place.

All at once Spooks toppled forward and my head snapped back as the ground beneath us disappeared. We hit bottom, landing in a jumble in a dry, but very deep, irrigation ditch. As I climbed up the bank, I felt more sheepish than hurt. The way Spooks kept his head lowered as we headed for home gave me the notion he felt the same.

⁂

There was always room in Mom's heart and at our kitchen table for the many people who spent time with us. The Searle family, comprising Dad's good friend George, a prominent attorney from Salt Lake City, and his children—Wayne, Ryan, Gweneth Gale (we called her both Gale and Gigi), and Tessie—found plenty of room.

Dad's other closest friend was Pete Parker, the pharmacist at Walgreen Drug in Rock Springs. Dad, George, and Pete spent countless hours with their heads together discussing problems and solutions, history and ranching. George, a single parent, saw summer days at the ranch with us kids and Mom and Dad as gifts to his children that their city life couldn't offer. And the Searle family became a gift to us.

Although our backgrounds could hardly have been more different, our voices blended easily in laughter. We didn't know that the day would come when Ryan would be a noted physician in the city of Boston. We only knew we were fascinated at the way he could pooch his stomach out until it resembled a watermelon. "Ok, you guys," he finally said. "I've got to quit doing that because it's starting to not go back!"

One time when they came from Salt Lake, they brought along Gale's black mare, Cindy. The pretty thoroughbred acted nearly overwhelmed with her new freedom, running with the other horses in the large pastures. Creek water seemed her greatest joy. Pawing at the glistening liquid, she splashed until she was dripping. Still not satisfied, she buckled her knees to lie down and let the water soak her.

Gale and I took a ride together, deciding to have a picnic on a sandbar near the river. We pulled the saddles off our horses' backs, figuring Cindy would head for the water the first chance she got. I was surprised when Spooks followed the mare into the river and began pawing. Then he lay down, dipping his mane into the water, imitating Cindy.

Gale and I pulled off our shoes, rolled up our pant legs, and took off running to join them. Spooks and I played together until we were nearly waterlogged, all thanks to a city horse.

When Dad hired Clyde Thompson, a young blond man from Vernal, Clyde instantly became a new family member. He first laughed out loud, then nodded with a grin on his face when I said to him, "Now, Clyde, please see to it that nobody tries to ride Spooks when I'm gone 'cause he's all mine."

Riding Chocko's brother, Brownie, Clyde cowboyed with us, teased us, and gave concern when we needed to talk. Sometimes he had his hands full in the bunkhouse keeping the rowdy gang of Bobby's teenage friends from Rock Springs in proper line. They laughed, joked, and wrestled. Clyde always came out on top, getting the boys to holler: "Uncle!"

When any of those guys were at the ranch, Mom and Dad could really get a lot of hay out of the fields and stacked in a hurry with the following promise: "If you kids get that hay hauled, we'll take you all to the rodeo in Vernal." The tractor blared, dragging the flat wooden slip across the cropped fields. Hay hooks were slung in all directions, stabbing into the heavy bales as layer upon layer filled the stack yards.

Nonie was strong enough to ride the moving slip, hook the bales on the ground below, and yank them aboard, one after the other. When I tried, the bale usually stayed put and it was me who was yanked, and I stumbled forward off the slip. Try as I might to navigate the slip and hold my mouth just right so I could snag one or two of those contrary things, I mostly just got in everyone's way. So I usually drove the tractor and then helped drag the bales off the slip so they could be stacked. It was hard, hot work, and it went on for a good share of the summer. But it bordered on fun when we had help.

Bobby and his group were *way cool*: Mike Kouris, whom Bobby called "Greek," was Bobby's best friend. Mom favored this young man with thick curly hair and brown eyes saying, "Mike's got a kind nature and he's level-headed." Others in the group were Bobby "Chopper" Cuthbertson, Bobby "Mouse" Gatti, Jerry "Moose" Clingan, Jim Martin, Steve Stark, Marty Compton, Sonny Francis, and Hugh Williams. Several of them often spent time with us at the ranch. We attended dances together at the Lodore School Hall. Sometimes the whole bunch of us teenagers wore matching western shirts.

The dances at Lodore were famous for their all-night fun. In Mom's youth, everyone arrived on horses or in wagons, bringing along food, hay, and bedding because of the long distances. There was a break in the dancing while everyone ate a midnight supper together, then they danced on until sunrise. Sometimes just after sunup, they were entertained by the cowboys riding a few broncs.

For us, many aspects of the Lodore dances remained the same as they had always been. We started getting ready early in the day. If a towel was hung over the window on the kitchen door, the men knew to stay out. Water was heated on the stove and poured into the metal washtub for bathing. When we were finished, the guys hauled the tub to the bunkhouse where they took turns filling and dumping the tub until everyone was scrubbed.

People from the surrounding area and towns came together just after dark to dance to the beautiful sounds of fiddles and guitars in that rustic building perched on a sagebrush hill overlooking the river and red cliffs of Lodore Canyon. When the children grew sleepy, pallets were made for them on top of old school desks against the wall or in a cozy corner on the oak floor. At midnight the music stopped and everyone dug into the food. Mom always brought extra for the band and anyone else who might be without. Our meal often consisted of fried chicken, potato salad, homemade buns that had been split, buttered, and filled with slices of bread-and-butter pickles, and large cinnamon rolls which filled the baking tins. Mom always made coffee in a huge coffee pot on a bonfire outside, offering it freely to everyone.

When the dances ended, a steady stream of cars and pickups headed to the different towns or to local ranches. Many came to our place and somehow managed to find a spot—whether it was a bed, a sleeping bag on the lawn, or even the cushion of a car seat—to get a couple hours sleep. Soon Mom and Dad were up, preparing breakfast and feeding ten or twelve bleary-eyed people at a time from stacks of hotcakes and platters of bacon and eggs until everyone was full. By early afternoon most everyone left for home as we, with the music still playing in our tired heads, usually climbed on our horses or drove to the hayfields. Whether we felt like it or not, there was always work to be done.

⁂

The first morning after arriving at the ranch for Christmas vacation my freshman year in high school, we woke up to find a couple inches of snow had fallen overnight. Shortly after breakfast, I hurried to catch Spooks while Dad, Clyde, Bobby, and his friends Mike Kouris and Jerry Clingan left to load the stock truck with hay and then feed the livestock.

The sky was blue and cloudless with the sun reflecting its subtle warmth off the new snow. Riding Spooks in the pasture just off the hill from the house, I could smell the sweet and bitter fragrance of the willows along the creek that were growing damp from the melting.

"Di-a-na," Mom called. I turned and saw her standing at the green-painted wooden yard gate. "While you and Spooks are just piddlin' around, will you do a little job for me?"

A couple minutes later I clutched a note for Dad in my hand and turned Spooks around. I spotted Dad and the boys in one of the lower fields. Some of the cows were still bawling and following the hay truck while most of the herd was settled in rows munching the cured alfalfa.

After crossing the creek and reaching the top of the bank, I nudged Spooks with my boot heels, saying, "Come on, fella, let's hurry!" Spooks broke into a gallop, leaving his tracks in the snow like a cookie cutter on dough. I stood in the stirrups, loving the feel of the motion beneath me. The air brushed tingles on my cheeks as I leaned forward into it. All at once the sky tilted and we hit hard. I shot out of the saddle, skidding and sliding before finally coming to a stop.

Barely raising my head with the wind knocked out of me, I saw Spooks was still down. Moments later, when I began feeling the cold hardness of the ice, I sat up. The huge ice patch had hidden itself well beneath the fresh snow.

Spooks groaned. I called out to him and watched him struggle to his feet. When I stood up, pain pierced my right ankle. Hobbling to him, I leaned into his shoulder and cried for us both. Somehow I got in the saddle and we made our way back to the fence near the house, where I yelled for Mom.

Mom hurried through the gate, saying, "Well, if this isn't a nice how-do-you-do. You look like a dyin' calf in a hailstorm."

Within a couple hours, Mom and Dad had me and my broken ankle loaded in the car. As we headed back over the one hundred miles we'd just traveled the night before, I felt guilty and sad, especially for hurting Spooks, to say nothing of causing all the Christmas plans to go haywire.

⚘

Our teenage years in Rock Springs revolved around school, drive-in movies, and dragging Main in shiny cars. Nonie's two best friends were Nancy Buxton and Kaylou Muir. My two closest were Beth

Pryich and Patricia Clark. We ordered cherry cokes and hamburgers from the Star drive-in and shared our romances and heartbreaks.

Mom made sure our home in town was inviting to all our friends. She cooked countless meals and made hot chocolate and popcorn. All the while she was biding her time, spending the twenty-three winters in town that it was going to take to get us all through school so she could finally stay year-round at the ranch where she longed to be.

❧

Early the next spring after I broke my ankle, we drove to the ranch in a chilly rainstorm. It was still sprinkling in the morning when I pulled on a jacket and walked to the pasture just beyond the corrals, anxious to give Spooks a hug around the neck.

When I spotted the horses near a grove of boxelder trees, I could see through the mist that all but Spooks had their heads down, eating. I felt a twinge; something didn't look right. As I got closer, I slowed my steps and called out, "What's the matter, boy?" His ears twitched forward, but Spooks barely raised his head.

Walking up to him, I saw that all four legs were terribly swollen from his shoulders and rump to his ankles. Several small holes dotted his legs and were oozing liquid.

I reached out and rubbed his soft forehead. Tears dripped onto my jacket, blending with the rain, as I took off my belt and put it around his neck. I had never seen anything like this. Clearly, he was very sick.

Barely tugging on the belt, I begged him to follow me, knowing I had to get him out of the rain. Just as he had for so many years, he tried his best to do what I asked, and in time we made it across the cruel distance to the corral, through the gates, and finally under the shed. Telling him I would be right back, I closed the corral gate and turned to run. I knew, because it had always been so, as I ran and ran that the kitchen would be warm, and Mom and Dad would be there and they would make him better.

It was concluded that Spooks had been struck by lightning. Dad gave him a shot of penicillin and I packed hay to him and filled a bucket with water. I spent as much time with him as I could over the weekend, and I hurried back to the corrals one last time before we had to leave for Rock Springs.

I was very aware of the gurgle in his throat as he breathed in and out. But he had eaten a lot of his hay. When he tried to drink, the water ran back out his nose and into the bucket, carrying with it strands of mucus. But I reassured myself, as I scooped the phlegm from the bucket with my hand and urged him to drink, that Dad was giving him penicillin, and he had, after all, eaten most of his hay.

The week of school in Rock Springs finally passed, and several of Bobby's friends came along in another car when we drove to the ranch. It was late when we got there, and after some jokes and laughter, the boys headed to the bunkhouse and Nonie and I climbed into bed.

We were laughing the next morning as we got dressed. Barely noticing the aroma of biscuits and gravy, coffee, and bacon, we were busy teasing one another about the boys. Just as I reached for the porcelain knob on the door leading from the living room to the kitchen, I heard Dad say to Mom, "Well, Spooks didn't make it."

I slowly opened the door and Mom and Dad turned to look at me. I screamed inside, *But you were giving him penicillin! And I made sure he was eating his hay!* But I heard my quiet voice ask, "Spooks didn't make it? He didn't make it?"

Mom drew me to her, to the steady warmth of her. "He was just too sick, honey. Dad did all he knew."

Later that morning birds were busy building nests, the warming air was awakening the bees, and I was settling into a much older world. After I stepped out of the screen door, I walked up the pathway, past the log storage building, and beyond the granary and shop. The first whiff of carrion was unmistakable.

Forcing one foot in front of the other, I continued along the old road. Finally I saw the white mound in the distance lying at the edge of the dump. The air was greased with the smell of death, but it didn't make me turn my face away because it belonged to Spooks, and I had to go to him.

Standing over the gelding I wiped my eyes. Everything around us was still except for the buzzing work of the flies, which I ignored. I tilted my head and looked into the gray dullness of a half-closed eye. There I saw Spooks as he had been, with black eyes gleaming and his mane of cream rippling on the wind. . . .

Slowly walking back to the house, I looked up when I heard a truck coming. Nonie was in the driver's seat and Bobby and the other boys were in the back. As the truck pulled up beside me, Nonie said, "We came back for you to come and go with us to feed. Come on, now, get your chin up and go along with us."

Climbing into the truck, I looked up and saw Bobby wink at me. After swallowing hard, I stuck my chin in the air. Nonie and Bobby, just about always, knew best. None of us realized, though, that our losses were only beginning.

Top: *Diana in front of the icehouse at the ranch with dog Lucky.*
Above: *Nonie sitting with Lucky in front of the icehouse.*

Bill at the ranch in 1961.

THE JOURNEY

Canada geese filled the sky with wing and song and then landed in our pastures to feed among the livestock. It was common in the evenings for three or four hundred mule deer to move silently from the cedars growing along the edges of the bench to dine on apples, leaves, and the many acres of alfalfa. All kinds of waterfowl and other wildlife continued to raise their young at the lakes. We heard rumors that officials from the Department of the Interior, federal Fish and Wildlife, and Utah Fish and Game were looking the ranch over with growing interest. Although we occasionally saw them in the distance and wondered, we were confident Mom and Dad would handle whatever came.

But soon the river ran red with poison as it flowed from the mouth of Swallow Canyon. Its sandy banks along the bottomland were speckled with silver bodies of dead and gasping native fish, sacrificed to make room for the trout that fishermen would prize. When the Green River eventually cleared, it ran cold and crystalline-clear through Brown's Park, never again to warm in the summer nor freeze in the winter. Government agencies and the newly constructed Flaming Gorge Dam had taken control of, and altered, the river's ancient personality.

In 1956, Congress authorized the construction of a number of main stem projects involving the Colorado River and its tributaries. Flaming Gorge Dam on the Green River, the largest tributary of the Colorado River, was one of several dams built with this federal authorization and in accordance with a 1948 compact between

Wyoming, Utah, Colorado, New Mexico, and Arizona to develop the waters of the Upper Colorado River Basin.

The construction of Flaming Gorge Dam began in 1958 and was completed in 1964; however, by 1962 major construction was finished and the dam had begun partial operation. The dam's purpose was to provide water storage, power generation, flood control, and recreation. As Flaming Gorge Reservoir filled, the river climbed the walls of magnificent mountain canyons and rose over large areas of countryside in Utah and Wyoming. The lake would come to measure nearly ninety miles in length and have more than 370 miles of shoreline. Flaming Gorge National Recreation Area, established in 1968, would soon be known to millions of people as one of the premiere fisheries and water-based recreation areas in the West. Below the dam for about fifteen miles, carrying into Brown's Park, countless rafters and trout fishermen would compete for space on the beautiful river.

While water development may have been essential, it didn't come without a price. From the beginning, both above and below the dam, drastic changes occurred. The natural rhythm of the Green River's flow was immediately negated. The river's quality and temperature were altered. Water released from the dam into the Green River to continue the journey to the Colorado River comes from the lake's depths, where the water stays at a constant cold temperature year around. A mixture of lime and other minerals in the glacial till that is picked up at the river's source in Wyoming's Wind River Mountains had cast the river in green for as long as man remembered. But in the lake environment, the glacial till settles to the bottom of the reservoir along with other sediment, leaving the water clear. The dam affected wildlife food sources and nesting and birthing habits. Selective chemical treatments that stained and poisoned the water eradicated native species of fish so non-native sport fish could be introduced. In general, long-standing ecosystems and habitats were greatly changed or destroyed. Wildlife and people were forced from their homes.

⚭

In 1964 Mom leaned against the kitchen sink and sighed. Gazing with glassy eyes over the top of the red geranium blossoms on the windowsill, she slid her hands into the soapy dishwater. Slowly shaking her head, she said, "I just feel so sorry for those folks from above the dam and what they had to face. All those homes, ranches, and beautiful places are gone, bought up by the government and flooded underwater."

Throwing the dishtowel over my shoulder, I rinsed the plates with boiling water from the teakettle and watched the steam rise from the worn dishes. Our sister-friend Velma, Clyde Thompson's wife, stood sad-faced while drying the center of the hotcake platter over and over again. She, Clyde, and their children would soon leave us to move back to Vernal to find work where they both had family. Nonie tugged on the glass door of the old dish cupboard and it rattled a little as it was inclined to do. I was taking more notice of such things these days.

"I heard that Charlie Crouse's daughter, Minnie Rasmussen, stayed in her home at Linwood until the water was rising," Mom continued. "Then she burned the place down herself instead of letting the government destroy it. Once upon a time, Minnie was the belle of Brown's Park." Mom shook her head again and tears filled her eyes. "I guess those birds in control are gonna have to have it all before they'll be satisfied."

Turning to look at each one of us, she said, "We're going to make it through this, girls. We're just going to have to sit down and have a talk with ourselves and toughen up."

⁂

Recently, arrogant men wearing dark glasses and representing our own federal government sat at our kitchen table. They drank coffee from our cups and ate warm banana bread, even as they made threats, brandished the weapon called eminent domain, and cut pieces of us away.

The men also sat at Uncle Jesse's table. He was the first to give in and sell. Then, under the heavy threat of eminent domain—a right of the government to take private property for public use—along with the promise of an expensive and useless court battle, Dad relented. As we stood in a murky cloud of denial, dismay, and anger, our ranch was sold outright—for a modest price determined by the government—to the federal Fish and Wildlife. The ranch would eventually be the location of the Brown's Park Waterfowl Management Headquarters. We were given a year to move.

Having graduated from high school in the spring, Nonie decided to spend this last winter at the ranch with Dad. With plans in a year to marry her high school boyfriend, she concentrated on her life to come. Climbing on Chocko to work cattle on a snowy slope, or watching the steamy breath lift from the frost-covered cows as they bawled for the hay she was about to feed, she tried not to think too much about the reality that time at the ranch was rapidly sifting away.

Nonie's long-time friend from Craig, Colorado, Norma Gardner, came and stayed with her for a few weeks. Dark complexioned, Norma had long black hair and grew up working cattle with her Dad on their land on Douglas Mountain. She happily helped Nonie with the ranch work.

One day the two girls were on horseback gathering a small bunch of cattle just up from the swinging bridge next to the river. They didn't realize a ground cover of weed stubs and coarse grass had spread a veil over a nearby strip of melting ice. When an ornery cow took off, Nonie and Chocko bolted after her. Suddenly Chocko's feet went out from under him, and he and Nonie fell on the ice. As they slid, splashing through the ice water, the grass and weeds clawed and stabbed.

Coming to a stop and holding back tears, Nonie was concerned only for Chocko as she watched the gelding make it to his feet. She patted him on the neck and gathered the reins. She walked with a limp as she led him off the ice. Soon she decided nothing but their pride was truly hurt, so she climbed back in the saddle. Away they went, loping up the hill through the rocks and sagebrush to head off the cow.

A few minutes later Norma said, "Maybe you'd better head back to the house and change. You're bound to freeze being soaked with that water."

"Oh, that's okay," Nonie answered. "We've got to get these cows taken care of before dark." Shivering a little, she grinned. "Besides, I'm only wet on one side."

About halfway through the winter, Nonie's good buddy Nancy Buxton came from Rock Springs to stay a week at the ranch. She ran her fingers through her short blonde hair and looked around, knowing she was allergic to just about everything that the ranch had in abundance. She began taking pills and dabbed at her stuffy nose with tissues.

The morning after Nancy arrived, Nonie couldn't believe it when her friend bent over to pick up her first bale of hay and immediately popped her thumb out of joint. Laughing and crying at the same time, she barely let Nonie close enough to see the awkward lump before Nancy yanked it back in place.

The next day Nonie backed the truck up to the tall haystack and said, "Okay, now, you climb to the top and roll the bales off to me so I can load 'em in the truck."

After she struggled up the side of the haystack, Nancy made it to the top and bent to move a bale. Suddenly she squealed, dropped the hay, and hurried backward. "There's a mouse under there!"

"Aww, come on, Nanc. We haven't got all day, ya know. Roll that thing down off there."

Nancy stuck her nose in the air, shook her head and said, "If that mouse wants this haystack, it's all his!"

The girls later decided to take a ride on the horses, so Nonie got them in the corral and bridled both Chocko and a horse for Nancy. Nancy walked up to her horse and barely touched him before she began to swell.

Looking her up and down, Nonie said, "Good grief, Nancy, you're puffin' up like a toad! You'd better get away from these horses before you pop."

After Bobby arrived he took over the job of feeding and asked Nancy to be his driver while he fed the hay from the red stock truck. Once they got into the field, the bawling cows surrounded the truck. Nervous about the job, Nancy scooted across the lumpy seat to get behind the wheel while Bobby climbed into the back. He cut through a couple strands of baling twine with a hunting knife and hollered, "Okay, Nancy, just take it easy and zigzag back and forth across this field."

Putting the truck in second gear, which to Nancy seemed the reasonable thing to do, she grabbed the wheel with both hands and slowly took her foot from the clutch. Moving across the open field, she could see in the side mirror that piles of hay were falling to the ground. She relaxed and began to feel pretty proud of herself. Wanting to make sure the engine didn't die, she pushed a little harder on the gas pedal.

Nancy didn't know that in the back of the truck Bobby was doing his best to stay upright while still managing to get some of the hay out to the cows. The speed of the truck bumping across the field had Bobby stumbling over bales and falling every which way. He was not pleased.

Nancy was looking straight ahead when she heard a noise at her side window. She jerked her head around and saw Bobby walking at a fast pace beside the truck while tapping the window with the six-inch blade of the knife. Nancy brought the truck to a stop, then rolled the window down.

"Nancy!" he said, looking squarely into her startled eyes and shaking the knife to emphasize his words. "Keep your foot away from the gas pedal and put that gearshift in *granny* and leave it there!"

By the time they got back to the house, Nancy was still wide-eyed but ready to laugh at the tale of the ominous tap at her window that made her toes curl and her hair stand on end.

Nancy got several bruises and lost weight during her stay at the ranch. But with the help of her medication, she did get to ride horses. Throughout all her ordeals, she never lost the clever wit that kept Nonie belly laughing.

I was fifteen by then and it pleased Mom that I volunteered to spend many weekends in town that winter, sitting at Grandma Taylor's bedside and doing her errands. Otherwise, even though Grandma had a housekeeper, Mom would have felt uneasy about leaving town to go to the ranch. Grandma was often cross and demanding. But Mom was dutiful, and I understood. As I watched Grandma's life slowly become a whisper, I was never sorry for the time I spent with her. In the end, Nina Taylor, the woman who traveled with her young family into outlaw territory to build a dream ranch, opened her eyes, smiled, and died peacefully at the hospital with Mom at her bedside.

Bobby graduated, Nonie married and left to get acquainted with her new life, and more of the truckloads carrying our lives away from the ranch disappeared around the bend of the rocky hill. Upriver, on Bake Oven Flat, a new mobile home waited for us on fifty acres that Dad managed to hold back from the sale.

Dad turned fifty-two that July, and Mom turned fifty a month later. Now, after all their years of hard work and sacrifice, they were facing an uncertain future. They considered moving away from Brown's Park, but that was almost too painful for Mom to think about. She nodded her head and cried when Dad promised her that if they could figure out how to keep the headquarters of Allen Livestock in Brown's Park, he would one day build her a home that would overlook the river.

Though the site on Bake Oven was growing only cottonwoods, cactus, greasewood, and sagebrush, we took some comfort that we had corrals there and it was just a short distance upriver from where Mom grew up. Also, it was next to where Bridgeport once stood and where Grandpa and Grandma Taylor parked their covered wagon when they first arrived.

⚬⚬

Mom and I were alone at the Brown's Park Livestock Ranch when I watched her put on her Stetson for the last time. She'd worn it for years, making it a familiar part of her. The cowboy hat had served her well, whether she was baling hay on the bench, riding Montan along a hillside on a rainy morning, or picking rosy apples in the fall.

"Let's take a walk, hon," she said.

Together we climbed part way up the rocky hill. In silence we turned—and we looked into the tranquil face of beauty.

I was trying to memorize everything about the shadowed cliffs and cedar-hidden places that had always offered so much, when Mom took me in her arms. Holding my mother tightly, I felt her tears on my cheek. My tears swam with hers and I finally had to believe that no miracle was coming. The government men in dark glasses weren't going to change their minds; they were never going to step aside and give the ranch back to us. Our time here was finished.

Making our way down the hill, we slowly followed the road across the bridge while admiring the wild cucumber vines that embraced the trees along the creek. We listened to the rush of the water and breathed its cool fragrance. After we walked up a little hill, we passed the shop where Dad had so often repaired the tractors and done the welding and past the metal granary and log storage building. Each one stood vacant now.

Following the pathway, we walked by the log home that had absorbed decades of history and years of our laughter. I couldn't stand to think of its emptiness, of the geraniums missing from the kitchen window, of the hollow sound our footsteps made on the freshly scrubbed floor. I wondered who would take care of the hollyhocks and honeysuckle and the old apricot trees.

The barnyard was silent without the chickens, turkeys, guineas, and peacocks that, except for a few peacocks, had all been given away. There was no place for them on Bake Oven Flat.

When we reached the corrals, Mom climbed part way up the poles as I leaned my forehead against the weather-softened wood. Here Charlie Crouse, Butch Cassidy, and so many others rode broncs and worked stock just as our family had. As my tears came again, I watched Mom take off her hat and hang it on the top of a high post. Speaking quietly she said, "Maybe this'll haunt 'em." Then arm in arm, we walked away.

⁂

The sun went down and the moon came up, changing from crescent to full and back again. The universe was in rhythm, but the world was out of step. The shock of President Kennedy's assassination was still new; race riots and protest marches were in the news along with reports of our troops under attack in Vietnam. The draft was in full swing as forces sent to Vietnam steadily increased in number. Two of our friends, Sonny Francis and Marty Compton, were in a car wreck on the new interstate highway on the outskirts of Rock Springs, forever altering their lives. While Sonny dealt with devastating injuries, Marty, who had been driving, dealt with the guilt he felt even as he was drafted and sucked into the horrors of war. Sad times continued as we learned that another from our group, Jim Martin, lost his life in a motorcycle accident.

Bobby's best friend, Mike Kouris, was drafted into the Army. Mike, whom I had come to know as the nicest guy I had ever met, left me polishing his class ring and writing him each day.

Before Mike's basic training at Fort Bliss, Texas, was complete, he found himself among hundreds of soldiers living in tents in an open field outside of Chicago where the wind, grainy with dirt, howled day and night. Mike and the other young soldiers were issued shields and other riot gear. There would be no bullets, they were told, and the bayonet covers were never to be removed from their rifles. They were trained to move shoulder to shoulder and be prepared for swarms of war protestors from their own generation launching an onslaught of sticks, bricks, rocks, bottles filled with urine, bags of feces, and screams of anger. Mike wrote in a letter to me that he was so very relieved when word came that the Chicago police were able to keep the protestors at bay and the soldiers would return to base.

Just a short time later, dressed in his uniform, Mike cried as I stood beside him at a crowded funeral. His close friend Steve Stark, a medic, was killed tending to the wounded on the battlefield in Vietnam, leaving behind in Rock Springs parents Jim and Anne, sister Kathleen, and his beautiful young wife, Nema.

ↂ

Back in Brown's Park, as was common practice with the places the government was rapidly accumulating, the historical significance of the Brown's Park Livestock Ranch was not considered in the least. Ownership of the land was divided between the Utah Fish and Game and the Bureau of Land Management. Our sweet log home was ripped apart and torn down; the corrals and outbuildings were bulldozed and burned. The creeks weren't used for any irrigation and were allowed to run to the river. The fields, most of the trees, shrubs, and flowers around the homesite, and many of the huge apple trees in the orchard died of thirst. Uncle Jesse's place was obliterated, and there was soon no evidence that a ranch was ever there. Weeds, however, found a good home.

As the higher-ups in distant offices made policies, irony hung in the air so heavily it was visible. The bench, where an apple orchard, alfalfa, and grain had attracted wildlife galore since the 1800s, was ordered left on its own. What had been a jewel of green from most vantage points across the valley turned to weeds and the color of straw—and supported almost no wildlife.

Dark, woody skeletons increased in number as the orchard died a slow death. While fields that were once lush died, a short distance away along the virgin face and foothills of Diamond Mountain, the BLM, with the cooperation of the Utah State Division of Fish and Game, carried out a plan it said would encourage more grass to grow and improve wildlife habitat.

After workers hooked massive chains between two bulldozers, the cedar railing began. Clanking metal and noisy engines couldn't drown out the moans as gnarled cedars and their young were ripped from the earth. Dust clouds boiled into the air as rock, brush, and pine tumbled along with the cedars. Artifacts fractured and crumbled as the remains of primitive Native American encampments were quickly destroyed. In the end, grotesque heaps of slab rock and boulders along with large piles of limbs and trunks littered the countryside where nothing familiar about the ancient campgrounds remained. It was so hard to watch.

Mom was tirelessly gathering history while desperately working for recognition and preservation of places not already destroyed. She gave talks and conducted large tours through the valley. All the while she and Dad worked together to develop the place on Bake Oven Flat.

It sometimes seemed that the journey was too far. Though, in the shade of the cottonwoods, Mom made the most of everything she had to create a warm and inviting place where her kids, grand-kids, neighbors, and others could gather, I saw her eyes. I saw them when she walked by the kitchen stove from the ranch where it now sat wrapped in a tarp beneath a tree, ovens cold, deteriorating; I saw her eyes as predators quickly picked off her peacocks one by one; I saw her eyes as dust storms tore at the laundry on the makeshift clothesline and peppered the metal siding on her trailer house home. Throughout the journey I saw her eyes—and she saw mine—as we were fed but a taste of the injustice heaped upon the fires and graves of the Indian people who, since some olden time until not so long ago, called this valley theirs....

Bobby during the Allen family's first autumn at Bake Oven Flat.

Bob at the Red Creek Ranch.

EVERY MILE HE RODE

He was now most often called Bob or R.C. Our brother's twenty years had gradually darkened his hair from blond to brown; his blue eyes were steady and trained to spot wildlife and cattle hidden in the far distance. In 1966, Mom and Dad leased the Patjanella Ranch east of Brown's Park, and he moved there with the responsibility of running it. Lucille, Charlie, Les, and Nonie were all married and living their lives away from the ranch. Bob was taking the reins, and he was riding on ahead, into our legacy.

It was the year before, during the first fall after we left the Brown's Park Livestock Ranch, when I, at sixteen, saw Bob, almost nineteen, as I never had—I saw him as a man. With Nonie living in Rock Springs, Mom, Dad, Bob, and I were left to gather the cattle from the meadows and draws on Cold Spring Mountain and get them headed to lower country before winter. We still owned the summer range on the mountain because it wasn't technically part of the Brown's Park Livestock Ranch. Although the entire herd of our breeding stock horses had been gathered and sold, we had been able to hold on to most of the saddle horses and all of the cattle.

Riding through the aspens and pines, Dad, Bob, and I bunched the cows and calves into one large herd. Mom drove a truck along behind as we started the cattle toward Little Beaver Meadows.

The sky grew dark and heavy with clouds building in a hurry. As we pulled our jacket collars around our necks, there was little more than the bruising of the sky to warn us.

The storm slammed into the mountain and its roaring wind battered us with chips of ice. Then heavy snow rode the wind and splattered and coated trees, cattle, horses, and us.

Mom hollered to me through the window. "Get in this truck and warm up and we'll take turns."

I soon took the offer. Mom left me to drive as she got on my horse. A little later I traded off with Dad and so on. There was one of us, though, who never once returned to the truck. Climbing on my horse, I went to find Bob. Struggling to see through the blizzard, I spotted him at the edge of the herd and called to him from behind.

"You'd better get to the truck and get warm, hadn't ya?"

When he turned and shook his head, telling me he was fine, the sight of him startled me: a layer of ice and snow at least an inch thick clung to the side of his face. It ran from just beneath his black cowboy hat, down his sideburn, and along the jaw line to his chin. He had no concern for it. Moving away at a trot, Bob and his horse were framed within the raw beauty of the storm. I knew he was where he belonged, heart and soul. He was a cowboy.

He met Betty Barger in college. Their time together was as brief as it was intense. The courtship, wedding, birth of Robby (Robert Carl Allen, Jr.), and the divorce happened before Bob could catch his breath from the day he met and fell in love with the energetic brunette. Just two weeks after Robby's birth, Betty told Bob that the life he loved, overseeing the Patjanella Ranch, was not where she belonged and took their son and left, soon moving to California.

Bob handled the pain he felt in silence, for the most part, except for the night when he went to sit at the side of Mom and Dad's bed. I watched in tears from across the room as Mom reached her arms out to him. Bob leaned into her and wept for what was never going to be and for the broken place inside him that would never completely heal.

One morning, not long after that night, Bob rode alone through the cedars along the ridge of a hill at Patjanella. He was following the tracks of the small herd of cow horses he had turned out a couple of weeks ago and now needed to bring in to the corral. The tracks and fresh manure appeared to Bob to be no more than a couple of hours old.

After coming to a stop at the point of the hill, Bob looked off the ridge. "Oh, no," he whispered. About halfway down the hillside he could see the dark and motionless body of a horse. Bob nudged his saddle horse forward, but the gelding was suddenly frightened by what lay below. With his ears pointed forward, Bob's horse snorted and jumped sideways.

Bob calmed his horse before stepping off him and tying him to a cedar. Then Bob walked down the slope and stood beside the crumpled form. He squeezed his sad eyes shut as he lowered his head. Bob could tell by the signs in the sandy dirt and the way the horse was lying that the gelding had been running off the hill with the herd when he collapsed mid-stride and died. Bob had known at first glance from the top of the hill that the horse, lying forever silent within the brutal and beautiful soul of nature, was Chocko.

It was Mom who softly prepared Nonie in the best way she could before she told her dark-haired daughter about the ending of the life of the horse that had been the jewel of her childhood. As Nonie gripped the edge of the kitchen countertop, leaned forward, and cried, there was no exact explanation Mom could offer for the cause. She told Nonie that Bob believed the heart in Chocko's mighty chest had simply given out. Through Mom, Bob sent his sister the reassuring words that there was no indication that Chocko had suffered, none at all.

The next spring, in 1967, an overpopulation of coyotes stalked our cattle. Time after time, they attacked the newborn calves. In spite of the frantic defense by their mothers, the dewy-eyed calves were yanked to the ground and killed.

Riding across a sagebrush flat on the Patjanella Ranch range along the Snake River with neighbor and friend, Bobby Sheridan, Bob saw a coyote trot boldly from the brush, barely concerning itself enough to glance their way. In an instant Bob was making a loop with his lariat and had his tall palomino cow horse digging her hooves into the ground and stretching out on a dead run. The coyote whirled and dashed away.

Sailing across the flat, the thoroughbred mare had her ears back and was gaining on the coyote with every stride when all at once a front hoof dipped into a hole. The mare's face hit the ground and she and Bob were thrown end over end. As they rolled into their third somersault, with his feet Bob pushed the mare on over and off him.

Skinned, dirty, bloodied, and sprained with his shirt torn half off, Bob slowly got back on the roughed-up mare. Feeling a prickly stinging, he said, "Looks like there's only two patches of cactus on this whole flat and I managed to hit them both."

With his shoulders hunched, Bob tried to hold off some of the hurt. The six-mile ride back was torture. Though his friend hurried on ahead, by the time he returned with a truck, Bob was saved from only about a mile of the ride. When he climbed from the truck a few minutes later, he was stiff, hurting worse, and figuring he would have been better off to have stayed in the saddle.

When Dad arrived from Brown's Park, he found Bob sitting in a chair. He hadn't felt able to change his shirt or even wash the blood and dirt from his face. Within three hours Bob was in traction in the Rock Springs hospital with a sprained neck and two crushed vertebra. Dr. Kos pulled out as many of the cactus spines as he could but about those that were broken off, he said, "They'll work their way out in their own time." A couple months later, I was with Bob when he pulled a stick more than a quarter-inch long from between his eyes.

As time went on, Bob's friendship with Bobby Sheridan's older brother, Monty, became one of his most valued. Running wild horses was entertainment for Monty since he was a kid. He told Bob of a sorrel he rode that was so good at it that when running horses on a certain long sagebrush flat, Monty could rope a wild horse and throw it in the manner of steer jerking, jump from the saddle, hobble it, get back on the sorrel, catch up with the herd, and rope another horse before reaching the end of the flat. Bob rode with him enough to know that it wasn't bragging with Monty, it was fact. It was from Monty Sheridan, Harry Carr, Boyd Walker, and others that Bob gleaned methods and techniques that elevated and honed his skills as a top hand. It was from Monty that Bob learned about chasing wild horses.

Douglas Mountain is beautiful, but the terrain is rugged and water scarce in the sweeping draws filled with sagebrush and on steep limestone ridges covered with thick stands of cedar, spruce, and pine. We grazed cattle there for many years. Looking off across the Yampa River, we could plainly see the remnants of an unbelievably steep and narrow outlaw trail leading down to the river. The outlaws placed cedar posts in the ground in critical places along the trail so their horses would have something to lean into after jumping off certain drop-offs and would not fall off the canyon wall. No posse was ever known to follow. For a very long time, wild studs and mares had staked out their own trails and territory in this remote country and went about doing exactly as nature dictated.

The horses running free on Douglas Mountain were extremely wild. Most of the small bands were commanded by a stud and led by a dominant mare. The stud almost always ran alongside or in back of the herd except during critical times of danger when he rushed to the front to lead the escape.

For decades, cowboys from the area challenged themselves, the horses they rode, and the wild horses they chased as they risked serious injury or death in their pursuit of the horses. Sometimes the horses were roped on the run, other times the herds were maneuvered into corrals known as traps. Strategically placed, the traps varied in size and material. Some of the structures were very old.

Although it is certainly true that some wild horse runners resorted to ruthless and despicable methods, a strong majority of the cowboys had a love for the wild horses and wanted the bands to survive. They did their best not to injure the horses. Though the cowboys felt the thrill of the chase in their souls, the practice also served several purposes: it kept the horse herds culled and cleansed, allowing the feed and water to sustain the horses and also wildlife and livestock; it supplied the cowboys with some tough saddle horses with plenty of bottom; and it made the men a little money from the ones they sold. If a cowboy had permits to graze horses on the surrounding range, he sometimes branded the wild horses in order to lay claim to them, then simply released them, knowing that no one else would be able to take ownership of the animals.

The first time Bob ran wild horses, he was with Monty Sheridan on Douglas Mountain. Riding around the head of a rim, a herd of horses showed itself. The horses started moving, heading toward a nearby trap. Bob rode behind them at a trot, hardly believing the luck that the horses were heading into the extending wings that would surely guide them into the gate of the corral. But, suddenly, the horses hit hard on their front feet, turned, and the entire band darted passed Bob like water through a sieve.

Spinning his horse around, Bob considered going after the herd but soon pulled to a stop knowing it was too late. The dust hadn't cleared before Monty rode up.

"Just jig-trottin' along is for cowboyin'," Monty chided. "If you want to play with horses, you're gonna have to *move!*"

Bob hung his head and later said he'd felt smaller than a mouse, but he'd learned. There would be another day, he told himself, and he'd be ready.

About a week later Bob and Monty returned to Douglas Mountain. Both men rode hard and they got several horses into the trap. That night, Bob didn't sleep knowing he would soon lead one of the wild studs off the mountain.

The next morning Bob felt a weakness in his legs as he threw a loop around the stud's head and tied on by dallying the rope around his saddle horn. Monty moved out of the gate with his wild horse first; Bob followed, not knowing what to expect. Although the stud fought some, it wasn't until they traveled about a half-mile that he really threw a fit and yanked Bob and his cow horse into a cedar. Bob got mad; the uneasiness evaporated.

Taking control, Bob positioned his horse to jerk hard against the stud when he fought to go the wrong way. Mostly he rode behind, driving and maneuvering, sometimes turning him in circles to disorient and convince him to go a certain way. Making their way along trails and off ridges, they eventually arrived at Patjanella in good shape. From then on, running wild horses came natural to Bob. He learned and he savvied it. Though the horses had his respect, he would have no more fear of them.

Bob had three particular horses that had the greatest athletic ability, wind, and intelligence to run wild horses, but they each had their quirks. Sonny, a big sorrel, did great as long as Bob didn't do something to make him mad such as run him uphill. Apparently he hated to run uphill because that played him out, so he bucked.

About a tall, lean bay named Tanner, Bob said, "He's a heck of a horse, but if you ever get off-kilter or hung up on him, he'll kill you in an instant." His favorite of all was a nearly black thoroughbred-built quarter horse gelding named Hobo. Sometimes Bob and Hobo went the rounds because both had a temper and could be stubborn. But when Bob pointed him at a herd of wild horses, they became as one. Bob roped thirty wild horses off Hobo in just one winter and forty-two horses in all.

There were plenty of laughs to go along with the close calls. Bob told of running horses with Clyde Thompson and said, "Clyde left part of his ear hangin' on a cedar." And he laughed bent over when he told of the first time his good friend and by then my husband, Mike Kouris, joined him and Monty chasing horses.

Bob, Monty, and Mike brought a herd, including three studs, on a dead run toward a trap known as The Mousetrap. The trap was round, built with sturdy cedar posts and cable. An outer perimeter of posts leaned into the structure, fortifying its strength. The gate was framed with two high posts and a cross pole on top with a sheet of canvas attached to it. Wings of fence fanning outward from the gate guided the charging horses into the narrow gate.

Bob and Monty stepped off their horses, hurrying to close the gate by sliding several poles across the opening. Mike, the last to get there, stayed on his horse and yanked down the ragged piece of canvas and began flapping it to discourage the horses from heading back through the gate as they sped around the corral. Suddenly a big sorrel stud split from the racing herd, ran straight toward Mike, and jumped. The same instant Mike saw the stud's hooves leave the ground, he vaulted off his horse and ran. The stud, going high, collided with the cross pole and was knocked backward into the corral.

Laughing as he slid the gate poles into place, Bob hollered, "Hey, Greek, thought you were had, did ya?"

A minute later, Mike stood high on the gate fortified with a wooden stick in one hand and the canvas in the other. Bob and Monty walked toward the snubbing post in the center of the trap, getting their lariats ready as the horses rushed around them. Suddenly another stud, ears back and mouth open wide, aimed for Mike and leaped. Mike dropped the stick and flew backward. As the stud bounced off the gate, Mike spun in midair, landed on his hands and knees, and scampered away.

"Did you see the Greek, Monty?" Bob laughed. "How do you suppose he did all that in just one motion?" Joining in the laughter, Mike took his place on the gate for a third time. Waving the canvas, he was able to deter any more escape attempts.

There was always a lot to learn and experience when he was around Bob, and Mike thrived on the seasoning. Soon several wild horses wore Mike's brand. No times were ever more satisfying for him than riding and working alongside Bob. They had a lot of fun; the physical risks were a constant and natural part of it.

I found it amazing that Bob never budged when horses came at him as he said "like alligators." I asked him how he was able to stand his ground the way he did. He shrugged his shoulders and said, "I've just been lucky that the horses have always been the ones to back down. I don't have to tell you that pretty much every day of my life is a close call. I've got a lot to be thankful for."

Continuing to chase horses in their spare time, Monty and Bob ran some studs into the largest trap on Douglas Mountain. As the horses ran around the huge corral, the men tied two lariats together to rope one of the studs and snub him to the post in the center of the huge corral. But when Monty threw the loop, he accidentally caught one of the studs around the middle and the horse went berserk. The other horses went into a frenzy.

There was chaos with the horses streaking in every direction and crashing into one another. In the center of the corral, Monty struggled to keep hold of the rope and pull the horse out of the pandemonium while Bob scrambled to keep the slack taken up in the rope so they didn't get tangled in it. Everything happened so fast there was no time for fear. Both men stayed with their jobs until, finally, they got the roped horse separated. The others soon calmed.

Another day Bob and Monty got a horse down in open country, built a fire, branded him, and then took the rope off his feet to let him up. But as the two stepped back, Monty's spur caught in the horse's tail. Bob quickly grabbed the horse's head, holding him down until Monty used his pocketknife to cut his spur free. Both men shook their heads knowing that if the horse had made it to his feet, he would certainly have dragged and kicked Monty to death. From that time on, Bob and Monty took their spurs off before they made a run at any wild horses.

Making the chase more challenging, Monty and Bob singled out certain horses they wanted to catch. They named one that eluded them Paperface. Paperface was a deep red sorrel with a white face, four white legs, and a large white spot on his belly. They chased him on and off for three or four years. Once Monty was near Tepee Springs when he closed in on Paperface. He threw several loops but needed an inch or two more of rope as it skimmed the top of the horse's ears. Time and again it refused to fall over Paperface's nose. Once Bob got close enough to throw two loops before Paperface hit the cedars and got away.

Bob admitted that he got "a bit crazy at it" as running wild horses became his passion. Once when he was riding Hobo, a wild herd he was chasing ran up against a barbed wire fence and began jumping it. Barely slowing, Hobo followed and cleared the wire. Just as Hobo's hooves touched the ground, Bob's loop caught a wild horse.

During an open winter, after the cattle were fed and the other morning chores finished at Patjanella, Bob rode alone to Douglas Mountain several times looking for horses. He always carried two ropes. After finding a herd he started it moving, following the horses to the places where he knew he could get into them. Bob roped a horse on the run, dallied the lariat around his saddle horn, and pulled his horse to a stop. Bringing the wild horse up close to him, he used the other rope to reach over the horse's shoulder, catch it by the front feet, and tip it over before getting off to tie the horse down. Then, to lay claim to the horse, he built a fire and branded the horse with a metal dee ring, which he carried tied to his saddle. In the end, he either turned the horse loose or led it off the mountain to be sold or broke for a saddle horse.

Riding Tanner (the gelding on which he didn't dare get off-kilter), Bob spotted a bunch of horses and followed them from an area called Sawmill through the cedars on a back trail to Allred Rim. As the horses started to climb a hillside, a mare and stud jumped together onto a ledge just as Bob threw his rope. It sailed over both heads, catching them in the same loop. Bob, with the spare rope in his hand, jumped from the saddle, knowing what Tanner was bound to do. Indeed, the bay saddle horse whirled around and bolted forward. The rope tied to the saddle horn yanked with such force that all three horses were jerked backward, off their feet.

Bob ran to the stunned pair of wild horses and swiftly put his spare loop over the front feet of the stud, throwing a half hitch around them. He then jerked the other rope off its head while leaving the mare caught with it. Bob knew when the mare got to her feet, she wouldn't go far before the cedars and Tanner would stop her. Just as he figured, when the mare got up, she went around a cedar one way and Tanner went the other. Tanner held her there while Bob built a fire. Before long he had both mare and stud branded and turned loose.

The best wild horse Bob ever saw was a polished black stallion with a white stripe down his face. He was beautiful, fast, very wild, and smart, and he showed extreme stamina. Bob chased him on and off for five years but couldn't get near him on any of his best horses. Finally he felt success when he caught the black in a foot trap made with a rope and counterweight that did its job and slowed the horse down. Riding the thoroughbred mare he had once done somersaults with, Bob easily overtook and roped the stud. Bob knew this wasn't a horse to be dealt with in open country—it would be best to take him to the nearest wild horse trap.

The black stud forced air through his nostrils in long, rough snorts. Then fighting against Bob's rope, the horse jerked back, throwing his body from side to side. He reared and lunged, grunted and squalled. Bob fought him through cedars and pines and over sagebrush and rocks. It was a long and savage battle, but eventually the black settled down and took the lead, moving at a steady walk.

The stud stayed in front, walking quietly, as they made their way along a steep and narrow trail on the edge of a thirty-foot drop. In the lull Bob relaxed some to the rhythmic sound of the hooves. But the quietness was deceiving: rising quickly from the calm, destiny flashed and twisted as the black stallion suddenly gathered himself on the brink of the cliff—on the edge of his life—and jumped.

Tensing and straining every one of his own muscles, Bob felt the mare plant her feet and draw back just as the stud hit the end of the rope. Somehow the mare withstood the fierceness of the jolt and, with body quivering, held her ground.

There was nothing Bob could do but sit stone still as the black, tied hard and fast to the saddle horn, struggled as he dangled off the side of the mountain. Bob knew the slightest shift of weight, even to get the knife from his pocket, could be more than his horse would be able to handle. He waited in a nightmare of fear and suffering.

It was a slow death. Bob figured it to be close to thirty minutes before the black silenced. With his pocketknife, he cut the rope and released the weight. Bob got off the mare and reached out a hand to stroke her damp neck. He led her a short distance down the trail and into the shade of a pine tree where he loosely looped the reins over a bough. Then Bob began the climb downward that would take him to the bottom of the cliff. A few minutes later, profound sorrow, deep admiration, and guilt intertwined as he loosened the rope around the stallion's neck and pulled it gently off the magnificent head.

Though Bob never forgot the black stallion, time moved forward and he rode wide-open across the rugged countryside many more times. The emotion of the chase was so intense for him that he literally grabbed hold of his breath and forgot to let it go. Watching the loop settle over a horse's head was what allowed him to finally release his breath. Quickly dallying the rope, he heaved, pulling air into his lungs. This dance with nature was as much a part of what defined Bob as anything ever was. Like an eagle in flight, he knew perfect freedom. It was part of him and his way of life.

The time arrived, in 1971, when a law passed making it illegal to run wild horses, and the grace period for the ranchers to round up any carrying their brands expired. It was the end of a way of life for not only the cowboy but the wild horse as well.

Under government management, in many places, the horse herds quickly grew to such numbers that forage and water couldn't support them. Horses died lingering deaths of starvation and dehydration. Sadly and ironically, in other places, such as Douglas Mountain, all trace of the wild horse soon disappeared.

❧

Not long after Bob's first marriage ended, he remarried and in 1970 had a son, Rick. Bob had been presented with, and signed, papers giving permission for his other son, Robby, still living in California, to be adopted. Allen Livestock bought a ranch near Encampment, Wyoming, and Bob and his family moved there to manage it. Mom sometimes took care of things both in Brown's Park and at the Patjanella Ranch when Dad needed to be at Encampment.

Mom was in her perfect domain, saddling up and riding out to check the cattle and bringing in and taking care of any that needed doctoring. Seeing a couple of mother cows with swollen, engorged udders, she cut them and their calves from the herd and trailed them to the corral. One at a time she roped the cows and snubbed them to a post. The cows blew snot at her and kicked when she touched the swollen teats, but she worked until the cows were milked out and relieved of their discomfort. Once the teats were smaller and less tender, the calves could take over the job. No one who knew her was surprised that mom could handle these tasks on her own.

Once Dad, Mom, and Bob made the exciting decision to purchase the Red Creek Ranch, located just a short distance north of Brown's Park in Wyoming, they made up their minds to sell the ranch at Encampment and to let go of the lease agreement on the Patjanella Ranch. Because deep snow made roads in and out of the Red Creek homesite impassable in winter, no one would live there during the winter months. Each fall the cattle would be trailed northeast twenty-two miles to the winter ranch. In the winter, Bob would base out of Rock Springs, where his wife stayed with their son, Rick, while he attended school. There were usually a couple of hired men living in the old log house at the winter ranch. Bob would drive there daily or stay a few nights at a time when the work demanded it. Bob would check regularly on the herd of bulls wintering in Richard's Gap on the Utah–Wyoming border and drive often to Brown's Park to touch base and help Mom and Dad with different jobs. The ranch work Bob handled during every season was constant, demanding, and spread out over long distances, but all in all this was a very good setup. The headquarters for Allen Livestock, Inc., would remain in Brown's Park.

The Red Creek country with its mountains, meadows, creeks, badlands, and ranching and outlaw history was beautiful and alluring. It would one day become clear to Nonie and me that every mile Bob had ridden in his life was bringing him straight to this place.

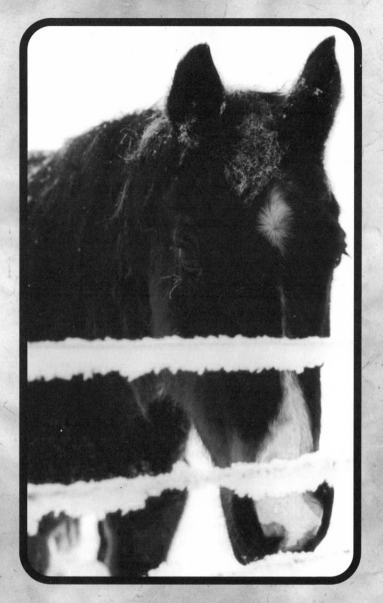

Above: *Hobo, Bob's favorite mount when running wild horses.*
Top right: *Bob and Mike Kouris at the Patjanella Ranch, Colorado, working on a steer's horns.*
Center right: *After they let the steer loose at the Patjanella Ranch. Shown is Bob Allen.*
Bottom right: *Mike Kouris on Douglas Mountain getting ready to brand his first wild horse.*

Marie in the fall of 1973.

SHADES OF GRAY

S topping at the table near the kitchen window, I looked out at branches that were bare and dark and forming intricate patterns on a sky pale with cold. Motionless, the trees looked down as if they understood why I cradled the small, worn box in both hands. *A few minutes more,* I thought, *and then maybe I'll have courage enough to open it....*

⚭

A lot of the cooking Mom did was without following any written guide. But she did have, and used regularly, a collection of favorite recipes. Some came from early day ranch women and others from her ancestors. Among those wonderful recipes were ice water cake, which Mom said never failed; a great-aunt's sour milk spice cake; a great-grandmother's potato salad; and Grandmother Taylor's applesauce cake.

Because blueberry was Bob's favorite, if she knew he was going to stop by, Mom's small kitchen sometimes filled with the smell of blueberry cobbler bubbling and browning in the oven. Mom and Bob's forks slid through the crust and berries as Bob asked her advice or told her the gist of how things were going with the cattle, fencing, irrigating, corral designs, and everything else at Red Creek. Though Dad and Bob often discussed the ranching operation, Mom and Bob occasionally found time for their own little visits. Lately they included stories that proved Red Creek wasn't breaking Bob in easy, such as his getting caught on a mountain after dark in an October snowstorm.

Still learning the Red Creek range, Bob rode all day looking for cattle on the top of Little Mountain. He'd misjudged the time it would take to get back to the truck and horse trailer several miles away at the Maxon Ranch. He watched black clouds gather and stir overhead, then urged his gray gelding to hurry as they moved downward by way of Trout Creek, through a steep canyon-like draw filled with huge pines, downfall, and underbrush.

Darkest night dropped across the mountain like a woolen hood, and large flakes of slushy snow began falling from the blackness. Unable to see, Bob got off his horse. He could hear the sound of the creek far below and knew they were near the edge of a sheer drop-off.

"Sometimes I pussyfooted," he told Mom, "then I'd smack into a limb on one of those big pines. Most of the time I was down on my hands and knees so I could feel my way."

The gray followed, usually keeping his nose near the ground just behind Bob's heels. Twigs and dead limbs cracked and snapped as the gelding pushed through the heavy timber.

Suddenly the darkness ignited. As explosive thunder pounded against the night, lanterns of lightning lit up the countryside. Back on his horse, Bob welcomed each flash as it arrived and showed the way. Soaked and cold, the tired pair made it to the truck just after one in the morning.

Scooping up the last of his pie, Bob said, "There were two feet of snow on the ground at Red Creek by morning."

Nodding, Mom answered. "Well, I know this much, getting caught out like that'll make a believer out of a guy. But I know you pay attention to your good common sense and I don't have to worry too much about you."

Later that winter Mom and Bob drove in a pickup from Bake Oven Flat and went as far as the snow-drifted road leading to the Red Creek Ranch would allow. From there they rode snowmobiles the remaining few miles to Red Creek, both for the fun of it and to check on the house. When Mom, wrapped from head to toe in warm clothing, fell off her machine and rolled down a fluffy hillside, she and Bob laughed together until tears ran down their faces. She was easy to laugh with, cry with, or just *be* with.

Getting reacquainted with the Red Creek rangeland was a happy time for Mom. It had long been her worry that she and Dad would have to leave the valley to replace the Brown's Park Livestock Ranch. Although the Red Creek Ranch was just a little more than ten miles from Brown's Park, none of its land lay near the river, and Mom felt confident that it wasn't in danger of being taken by the government. Purchasing Red Creek, a place she had known all her life and had ridden across on horseback, in buckboards, and then automobiles, meant the ranching operation of Allen Livestock, Inc., could finally come back together as a unit.

Without bitterness, Mom and Dad, from the beginning, welcomed the government employees and their families who moved to Brown's Park to oversee the different refuges. They grew especially fond of Neil and Merlene Folks, a young couple who moved into a new house constructed on the exact spot where our log home once sat.

Merlene, a petite and dark-haired young woman, was energetic, generous, and loyal by nature. Just like Mom. It was natural that their friendship would become an exceptionally close one. Mom was tickled to learn that Merlene had an ancestor connected to Brown's Park's outlaw history.

Describing her great-grandfather, James "Jim" Marshall, Merlene said, "I've been told he owned good, well-bred horses and that Marshall Draw up here on Diamond Mountain is named after him. But he was a heavy drinker and not a very nice man."

In the early 1880s, Jim Marshall and his wife sold their ranch in southern Utah to Butch Cassidy's family. Then the couple traveled with Butch Cassidy to Brown's Park. A few years later, when his son (Merlene's grandfather) was just ten years old, Jim Marshall was found slumped in his buckboard, having died of natural causes. Marshall was buried somewhere on Bake Oven Flat. Though Mom and Merlene searched the area for the grave, time had hidden the spot, and it left behind no clues.

❧

Mom continued working to preserve the history of the area: she gathered stories from her older brother, Jesse, who knew a lot of the old-timers and rode in the posse when John Jarvie was robbed and murdered. She also searched through files in newspaper offices; received information from museums and libraries; communicated with Butch Cassidy's sister, Lula Parker Bentensen; and welcomed Charlie Crouse's daughter, Minnie Rasmusssen, when Minnie came to visit and share her recollections. Involved with the Daggett County Historical Society and the National Association for Outlaw and Lawman History, she learned and taught.

When Mom heard that the Utah Fish and Game planned to destroy the buildings on the ranch where she was raised, she grew desperate to save at least the Parsons cabin built by Dr. John D. Parsons in about 1874. It had served as home and shelter for families and outlaws. With help from a Daggett County historian, Mom compiled the cabin's history and presented it to the Utah Historical Society in Salt Lake City. The next morning, January 13, 1972, Mom was told the cabin would be placed on the state register and saved from destruction.

I went with Mom to the Taylor Ranch just a few days before most of the buildings were to be bulldozed into piles and burned. As we walked up a steep road that was nearly gone, she showed me marks on the rocks left behind by her father's wagon wheels. She pointed out the sandy draw where one day when she was a teenager, her horse's hoof kicked up a glistening blackness. Looking down she saw an obsidian spearhead that measured seven or eight inches long. Because her dad taught her it was against the Ute people's belief to remove the arrowheads, she admired its beauty and left it behind.

Mom told me many stories of her childhood. She pointed out where the buffalo grazed and played in the far pasture and told me about bringing the milk cows to the barn at sundown. As we walked to each building, she spoke about the cellar, smokehouse, chicken coops, blacksmith shop, stables in the barn, and the small house built for her dad's mother who smoked a corncob pipe. She told me how her mother whitewashed the walls of the Parsons cabin when they lived there before moving into the new house. She explained the technique of rag-rolling her mother used to paint the walls of that beautiful home her father built. She described the way the geraniums bloomed red in the bay window of the dining room; the beautifully carved clock on the fireplace mantle; and how, in summer, wild roses completely covered the springhouse with sweet blooms.

It was late when we climbed to the top of a rocky ridge overlooking the once magnificent ranch. Mom turned to say goodbye to the deserted, dilapidated buildings and few remaining crab apple trees and flowering bushes. She lowered her head and squeezed her eyes closed. Then looking up, she tightened her lips together. She was so proud of the life she had known there.

After wiping her eyes with the palm of her hand, Mom turned and took hold of my arm. "I have my memories, Sis," she said softly. Then, just as we had the day we said goodbye to the Brown's Park Livestock Ranch, arm in arm we walked away.

In April 1974, mom's dream home, which would overlook the river, began to take form on Bake Oven Flat. By now apple, apricot, peach, and cherry trees had taken root there. Rhubarb grew huge stalks and raspberries and lilacs bloomed alongside a large vegetable garden. A new alfalfa field spread upriver and was sprinkled with cattle during the winter. Each of us, their children and grandchildren, visited often as did many friends and relatives. Mom had more time to devote to the history she loved. The book she hoped to write was often on her mind as was the museum she planned to establish.

One of Mom's greatest achievements for Brown's Park occurred on February 24, 1975. Three days before the Federal Fish and Wildlife was to destroy Lodore Hall, Mom was successful in having it placed on the National Register of Historic Places.

Built in 1911, the school/hall had continually served the community. Mom adored the proud old building where she had attended school, dances, and other social events held there in her youth and throughout her life. Mom was still active in the local women's club and helped with fundraisers for the upkeep of the building. But countless times through the years, Mom used her own money to replace broken windows or make other needed repairs.

Mom cried and laughed when she learned the building was saved. During this same time, she was making plans to host actor Robert Redford, author Edward Abbey, and others as they documented the Outlaw Trail for a feature in *National Geographic*.

Though Mom began feeling ill, she barely mentioned it and was eager to ride horseback with Bob whenever she got the chance. Clyde Thompson, who worked for Mom and Dad for so many years, was now living in Vernal with his wife, Velma, and their children. They often drove over Diamond Mountain to visit and help out. One morning Mom and Clyde were riding with Bob, gathering cattle in a large pasture at Red Creek.

As the cattle trailed toward the gate, Clyde turned to look over his shoulder and said, "There's a coyote." As he turned back around in the saddle, both Bob and Mom whirled their horses around and took off on a dead run.

Leaning forward, Mom gave her horse his head. Her eyes grew moist from the wind in her face and she laughed out loud. She yelled out a "Whoop!" as her horse cleared a ditch, they sailed onward, down the slope and across the long pasture.

When he reached the bottom of the field, the coyote ducked under the wire fence and disappeared into the sagebrush. Pulling her horse up, Mom was out of breath and grinning wide.

"Guess we showed that dirty bugger that he'd better stay outta here!" she panted.

"Yes we did, by golly," Bob laughed, as their horses trotted back toward Clyde and the cattle.

⚭

After living a few years in Laramie, Wyoming, Mike and I couldn't wait to take part in the ranch life at Red Creek for awhile. Dad, Mom, and Bob had offered us the opportunity to be part of the ranch operation. While we didn't know how long we would stay, there was no place we would rather be so the offer was irresistible to us both. I quit my job at the University and Mike quit his, teaching at Laramie High School. The news that we would have a child in early spring kept me out of the saddle but gave me time to spend with Mom and Dad while Mike rode and worked with Bob.

Together, Mom, Dad, and I watched construction continue on their new home. We worked the huge vegetable garden and picked chokecherries in Jesse Ewing Canyon. Then Mom and I made several quarts of chokecherry syrup. Later that fall, using her canning cookbook and recipes from her recipe box, Mom and I canned chili sauce, mustard pickles and beet pickles, stewed tomatoes, crab apple butter, pear and pineapple honey, huckleberry syrup, and orange-spiced peach and cherry jam.

Gently rubbing at her right side with the palm of her hand as I had often seen her do lately, she smiled. "We need to make enough for the whole gang!" Her *gang*—all her kids and their families—was accustomed to having Mom's canning to savor throughout the winter months. I would forever treasure this time with her.

A short time later, Mom was stricken with a severe gall bladder attack, and she went through a difficult surgery in Rock Springs. We each took turns at her bedside throughout the ordeal. We were told she would soon feel better than she had in several years. She did feel better, for a short while. But then she seemed to lose ground.

It wasn't going to be a hard day of riding, Bob told her. "If you feel up to it, we'll just take this little bunch over to Meadow Gulch."

Mom mounted a buckskin quarter horse named Joker. She told Bob she liked the gelding best: "He always stands still until I get on."

The pace was slow, following behind the cattle. But suddenly a cottontail darted from beneath a bush, startling Joker and causing him to jump sideways. The saddle horn hit Mom hard in the side of the abdomen. It hurt her worse than she said. It never again stopped hurting.

It was Easter morning, March 30, 1975, when our little Nicholas James was born. While I was in labor, Mom insisted on staying all night at the Rock Springs hospital with Mike and Nonie, though we had each gently told her she must get some rest. She was clearly very ill: her skin was colored dark with jaundice.

I would later learn she had postponed the exploratory surgery her doctor was set to perform because my due date was near. She was determined to first see me safely through my time of giving birth.

Four days after the baby and I got out of the hospital, I was busy bathing him at Mom and Dad's home in Rock Springs. Thinking about Mom, I wondered whether her surgery was over. I was certain the doctor was correct and it would simply be a matter of removing a blockage, probably a gallstone they missed earlier or perhaps scar tissue from the surgery before. I knew Nonie should soon call. She and Charlie were with Dad at the hospital and Lucille was on her way, driving to Rock Springs from her home in Green River.

Glancing out a window, I was surprised to see Nonie opening the yard gate. Then I saw the morning sunlight glisten on the tears covering her face. Panic rose in my throat to a scream.

⁂

At Red Creek, though the morning air was soft with a hint of spring warmth, Bob felt an uneasiness in the pit of his stomach. Mom was on his mind as he walked down the hill, heading to the corral to check on a cow that was about to have her calf.

The cow struggled throughout the morning, trying to give her baby life. The birth was complicated by problems, and Bob worked hard with her. Sweat was running down his cheeks when something caught his eye. His insides tightened when he recognized Mike's pickup making its way down the hill leading to the house. Kneeling over the cow, he continued his work.

Bob didn't look up when he heard the squeaking of the wooden corral gate as Mike slowly opened it. Mike stood in silence as Bob made the last pull on the calf, and the pretty little heifer slid into the world. Bob finally got to his feet and looked at his friend with eyes that were red-rimmed and fearful.

Mike's voice was weak when he said, "Your mom has cancer and only about four to eight months to live."

Clenching his jaw, Bob spoke through his teeth, "I knew it! I knew it!" Then the two young cowboys stood together and cried.

In the coming months Mom fought her battle, and we fought it with her in any way we could. With gentleness and strength, she put up an incredible fight against a spreading pancreatic tumor. She spent as much time as possible in her just-finished home beside the river, and we all spent as much time as we could with her. Of all the piles of cards and heartfelt wishes that came from near and far, one particular gesture stood apart.

Merlene Folks arrived one day carrying a bouquet of branches covered with fragrant flowers and buds. Lying in bed, Mom closed her tear-filled eyes and breathed the scent of her childhood. Merlene understood the depth of the meaning of her gift: she had carefully snipped the branches for her dearest of friends from a blossoming crab apple tree at the Taylor Ranch.

From the shattering time of his sister Nancy's death from scarlet fever in 1909, Uncle Jesse had kept a large part of himself in a distant place. Throughout his life he was often sullen. Although Mom loved her brother deeply and wanted to believe that he loved her, he offered her no more than a casual friendship. He had never shown her affection until the day he drove to Brown's Park from his home in Rock Springs to come to her bedside. There, all reservation and doubt between them ceased to exist.

As Uncle Jesse sat beside Mom, he held his small-brimmed Stetson in his lap with one hand and gently held Mom's thin fingers with the other. Their soft-spoken conversation went on for some time. When at last Uncle Jesse rose to leave, both his and Mom's eyes filled with tears. Uncle Jesse bent over and kissed his little sister's forehead, long and tenderly, and then they said good-bye.

As I walked Uncle Jesse to the door, he wiped his eyes and began to tell me a story. He pointed to the top of Mountain Home and told me about the day he watched Mom and Dad, not yet married, bring a herd of horses off the mountain on a dead run. Uncle Jesse shook his head and said he hadn't expected them so soon and wasn't in position with his horse to turn the herd as the three of them had planned.

"When Marie and Bill saw the horses were going to outrun us all and get away, they both brought their horses to a sudden stop, jumped off so they could yank their saddles off to lighten the load, then swung back on their horses and took off after the herd in a wild dust while riding bareback. Oh, how I admired the sight of them. I'll never, ever, forget it," he said.

As I stood at the door and watched Uncle Jesse's aging, dark green truck disappear into Jesse Ewing Canyon, I didn't know that this was just the first of countless and priceless stories he would lovingly and openly share with me. In the coming years we would sit together for hours on end as he told me about traveling in a covered wagon, the death of Nancy and how it affected him, early day life in Brown's Park, and the historical figures and events he knew firsthand. As for this day, I stood looking at Mountain Home and watched Uncle Jesse's memory come to life. There rode my dashingly beautiful father and mother, with their lives still stretching far before them. Then I clutched the story in my hands, held it to my heart, and cried.

During the month of October 1975, Dad arranged for Mom to fly home in an air ambulance from the University of Utah Medical Center in Salt Lake City so she could take part in the event when Robert Redford and his group were there. Although very thin and weak, with elegance she invited Redford to sit at her bedside for a private visit.

Arrangements for Mom to fly home were made again in November so we could all spend Thanksgiving together. Then in Salt Lake City on the eleventh of December, as Dad held tightly to her hand, Mom passed away.

We, her family, stood together at the cemetery as the bishop spoke to the large gathering. December's breath was cold and the sky endless in folded shades of gray. Before this, we had never once imagined the always warm, sturdy core of us to be vulnerable—as fragile as the flakes of snow swirling around us on the wings of the wind.

But just as the blue mountains of her valley would survive the winter and beyond, so would the mighty force created from her life as it flowed in soft waves, rippling onward. Mom, a ranch girl, who grew up in an old and remote part of the West, had a life-changing influence on countless people. Included were those of wealth and power and also the burdened, such as the Ute family she embraced and helped throughout the years. And because she always had plenty of room to tuck another gently beneath her wing, she soothed the injured places inside numerous young people, giving them a sense of self and belonging.

Decades later, Saturday, November 18, 2000, the following words were written to Nonie by her best friend, Nancy Buxton Strid.

⁂

... I know you know what that place means to you, I wouldn't even try to put it into words. I wonder though if you know how deeply the time I spent there affected me. In fact, when I look back at those years, I realize that old ranch house, while being your home and the family business, was a refuge for so many of us who were living in circumstances not

so terrific. I don't know if I can ever tell you how much those weekends away from my chaotic home life meant to me. But it wasn't only me. Think of all the kids who lived through the week knowing on Friday we'd pile into one of your vehicles and get away from town for a couple of short, ever so fast days.

I remember so many things. I remember sleeping through nights so cold the air almost froze coming out of you all piled together in that bed in that little bedroom. I remember that wood stove that felt so good to be near. I remember your Dad yelling, "Everybody up in there or I'm sending the boys in." Piling out of bed and pulling on our clothes in the dark frosty mornings. I remember breakfasts that were feasts. Meals cooked on that fabulous old stove that were delicious. And generous as your mom herself.

I remember hanging on for dear life in the back of the pickup bouncing across what had to be a newly plowed field on the way to feed cattle. I remember trying to drive that truck while you and Bob were trying to feed. I kept slipping the clutch cause I didn't know what I was doing, (as usual) and pitching you off the tailgate.

I remember trying unsuccessfully to keep up with you tossing bales of feed in to the back of the truck. I remember the first time on a horse. Getting on, getting off, and trying very hard to walk a straight line after, so as not to look like the city girl I was.

And I remember your wonderful mother. She was such a rare person. Among the things I most remember about her was her generous spirit and terrific sense of humor. She was so wise. She impacted my life in so many ways, and I doubt she ever knew or gave it a second thought. It was just the kind of person she was.

It was a privilege for me to be a small part of that marvelous place and time, and my life is richer for it....

⚭

A few weeks after Mom's funeral, Mike left for work and our small son slept in his crib. During the summer before, Mike had accepted a teaching job in Riverton, Wyoming, and we had moved there in August. Our new home, located in a pretty spot a short distance from Riverton, was quiet. Carefully I placed the small box on the kitchen table next to a waiting pen and stack of white cards. Slowly, with heart pounding, I reached for the lid on the recipe box

Mom had left me. Finally I tipped the lid back, releasing a rush of memories and aromas, mellow and sweet.

The recipe cards, some stained, others torn, were almost all in her handwriting. I could barely touch them for fear they, or perhaps I, might crumble. Finally taking a card from the box, I reached for my pen and began to copy it. I couldn't imagine the ranch without her recipes being there. I would copy each one and take them in a pretty new box the next time I traveled there.

Outside, the sun melted the sky, turning it deep blue. I worked on, visiting Mom in her kitchen time and again as stories were revealed as though the cards were pages from a diary. The motion, words, and rhythmic flow of the ink brought her beside me, urging me to heal.

A couple days later, when I was nearly finished copying the recipes, there came other nudgings, soft but persistent, to continue Mom's work as a voice of history. As time moved forward, I worked hard and did my very best to do her, and history, justice.

∽

And then, full circle, that's where Nonie, Bob, and I landed. We saddled our cow horses, buckled our chaps, and rode together once again.

Left: *Bill and Marie in their new home in the summer of 1975.*

Below: *Marie in 1974 with Bob in the background.*

Left: *James "Jim" Marshall in the late 1800s* (Courtesy Merlene Folks).

Below: *The Taylor home just before its destruction.*

Top: *Bob chopping holes in the ice to water the cattle.*
Above: *Diana at the Red Creek Ranch in 1972.*
Right: *Diana in 1974.*

Nonie and Diana
on Blue and Handsome.

ON SILVER MIST

It was September 1984, and Nonie and I bumped along in her pickup over the washboardy road leading to Red Creek because it was beginning—the two months of fall gathering. Mom had been gone almost nine years, and Dad was remarried to Ella Shiner, whom he had known since childhood. He often helped Bob at the ranch but spent most of his time at his home in Vernal with Ella. After several years of planning our lives around our homes and raising our young children, Nonie and I now planned the year around September and October. Our families lived just a horse pasture apart on ten-acre homesites, outside of Riverton near Kinnear, Wyoming. Each fall we could hardly wait for Bob to yank us back into our favorite world filled with bumps, bruises, saddle sores, storms, bogs, sunburns, spicy sagebrush dust, coyote yips, tears, laughs, bellowing bulls, and chestnut winds blowing from the herds.

Bob stood at the yard gate of the log ranch house grinning as we pulled to a stop. "It's about time you girls got here."

Nonie stuck her head out the window. "Did ya miss me?"

Looking sidelong, Bob grinned and said, "Yeah, I missed ya—just like a sore thumb. Come on, you two. Soon as we get your stuff unloaded, we gotta ride to Tepee to hunt for yearlings. I've pretty much cleaned that country, but I know I didn't get all of them."

Stretching our bodies, stiff and tired from the long trip, Nonie squinted and moaned, "Can't we at least have one cup of coffee first?"

"Okay, but don't blame me if we don't get back before dark. See those clouds over there? We're probably gonna get wet. And I've got three new horses to ride that some people in Rock Springs have been having trouble with, that I need to see if I want to keep. So, we might have fun."

Nonie rolled her eyes. "Oh, that's just great, Bob."

The screen door slammed shut as they went into the house lugging suitcases and still yammering back and forth. Tilting my head back, I closed my eyes and sniffed the air that was filled with both the scent of the ranch and the coming rain. I thought about Mom and knew she was smiling.

Within thirty minutes we had swigged a cup of coffee, put on our chaps, boots, spurs, and hats, had our yellow slickers tied on behind the saddles, and were mounting Bob's tryouts. We hadn't made it past the corral when Nonie stopped her white gelding.

"Bob, I don't like the feel of this horse and I'm not riding him. I've got a bad feeling here."

"Really?" Bob said. "Okay then, let's trade and I'll ride him."

I was fine with my palomino gelding called Nanner until Bob said he ran away with Dad a couple of days ago. Ran away with Dad? Though he was in his seventies, he was still one of the strongest men I knew.

"And watch what you're doing with this sorrel, Nonie," Bob told her. "He was being used as a barrel horse until he got bad about grabbing the bit in his teeth and running away. I don't think either of you girls should go any faster than a trot until you really get a feel for these horses."

After riding across what was called the big brush pasture, the three of us split up, each taking a different draw with plans to meet where the draws come to a head on the side of Tepee Mountain. Nanner's gait felt good beneath me. The leather saddle I'd had since I was a teenager made soft creaks as he stepped around the brush and onto the trail we would follow up Tepee Springs draw.

Everything about this time and place felt comfortable and as it should. My chaps were broken in and molded to the shape of my legs. A while back Bob gave both Nonie and me pretty silver bridle bits, and my beautifully engraved spurs were a present from our cousin, Allen Taylor, a superb silversmith. The first time Bob saw my hat, a gift from Nonie and her daughter, Ginger, he grabbed it up and said, "You need a big hat shaped like Grandpa Taylor's." Holding it over the steam coming from a teakettle, he shaped it so the crown sat high over a wide brim. I adored it.

Cloud shadows slid across the creek banks passing over mossy rocks and the blue-gray berries hanging in clusters on the cedars. As Nanner took me in a fast walk and sometimes a trot along the trail, sagebrush branches spun the rowels of my spurs, causing them to sing. I thought about long-ago cowboys and outlaws riding this trail, hearing the same melody. I was reminded of the story Mom told us of the shooting of Willie Strang, which happened here at Red Creek in 1898. We often rode past the graves of Willie Strang and Valentine Teters.

Much later, I raised my eyes and spotted Bob in the distance as he rode the white gelding out onto a point of Tepee Mountain. It was a powerful sight.

So many times Nonie and I had seen Bob stop his horse on some high ridge, cross his wrists on the saddle horn, and look across the vastness for cattle. This rangeland he oversaw and rode horseback across is immense and rough. In a time of anti-ranching politics and disappearing ranches, he'd remained determined. But through years of white cold, heat that seared the skin, sunsets, and change, he'd been through a lot. We watched, sometimes with wonder, always with pride, as the fulfilling but tough and dangerous work he did and the country he rode chiseled him into the man he had become.

A soft rain was falling when I joined up with Bob, and we both were wearing our slickers. Neither of us had seen any yearlings.

"I thought Nonie would be here by now," he said. "But I know about where she has to be so we might as well head that way." Bob took the lead and I followed him down the steep slope.

We stopped our horses in the meadow at June Spring. A thick stand of aspens and pines sweeping upward and over a ridge wore a beautiful mantle of silver mist. The high-pitched call of a bull elk drifted from some hidden place within. When Bob answered the exquisite sound with whistles that spoke so clearly of his skill and relationship with nature, the beauty of it sang to me. Again and again they called to each other, with the sounds gliding through the trees on the mist.

When we turned to leave June Spring, there was so much I wanted to say: I wanted to tell Bob how truly magnificent he was at times like these; that he sat a horse more handsomely than anyone I'd ever known; how grateful I was to him for all the years of hard work that kept our heritage alive; that he had just now given me a gift—a pure and perfect moment in time. But because the words did not come, I didn't say them, and he never knew.

We were glad to see Nonie and the sorrel when they came into view on the skyline of a tall hill. She'd found no yearlings either. All three horses had, so far, been well behaved. As the rain stopped, then started again, we rode cross-country through draws and gullies and over rocky hills to a barbed wire fence.

"It's getting late," was all Bob said as he turned his horse down the fence line and broke into a fast trot. Nonie fell in behind him. Leaning forward and standing in the stirrups, I followed.

The countryside and fence posts sailed by as Nanner and I both puffed on the sweetened air. The dampness felt satiny and cool on my face, and the rocks and sagebrush were shiny from their fresh scrubbing. On and on we went at a quick and rhythmic pace. After wondering if Nonie's knees hurt as much as mine, I did my best to forget the ache of fatigue. Sometime later I got my magical second wind and the hurts grew numb as the jarring motion became fluid.

Suddenly Bob pulled up on the reins. Turning in his saddle, he said, "Hey, we didn't get skunked after all. There's three yearlings up ahead."

After gathering the red heifers, we started them down a trail through the cedars at a walk. We were still a couple hours from the house, but driving three calm heifers was bound to be a snap.

The three of us had plenty of time to relax and visit until we reached the gate leading into the little brush pasture near the house. As it began to pour, the rain ran off the front of our hats in a steady stream as Bob went ahead to open the gate. When he rode past them, the heifers spooked and took off. That was when the circus began.

We weren't on a level sagebrush flat. This hilly spot was littered with crevices, gullies, big rocks, a deep wash, a bog, and plenty of brush and cedars. Nonie and I both knew Bob was right: it would be dangerous to let these horses get going too fast. Instead of dashing after the cattle as we would normally, we went in a trot, bobbing along after them. The yearlings soon stopped, but we didn't. These weren't cow horses. Not understanding what this whole business was about, the geldings were quickly wound up and hard to handle.

Crisscrossing, Nonie went one way, I went another, and the yearlings spooked again, splitting in three directions. Each time Nonie and I passed by the bewildered heifers, they stopped and watched us. Glancing over my shoulder, I saw that Bob was still back at the gate with his horse spinning and jumping sideways.

All of a sudden Bob and his horse shot by us at a dead run. The white gelding's hooves clattered loudly on the rocks as the pair disappeared over a hill.

"Bob! Bob!" Nonie called. "The yearlings are over here."

"I don't think he's looking for us," I called back. "He's having trouble with that horse."

Back over the hill Bob and the gelding charged, again scattering the heifers before disappearing into the cedars. Neither Nonie nor I had much time to think about what was happening with him. The job always came first. We'd worry about picking up the pieces later.

I let Nanner into a lope, determined to get in front of the yearlings to get them turned. Pulling on the reins, I soon knew I'd made a mistake. Instead of slowing, Nanner kept picking up steam. Sailing past the lead heifer, I grabbed a rein in each hand. Just as the palomino lunged to jump a young cedar, I pulled straight toward my hips as hard as I could. Nanner shocked me when he stopped mid-stride, mashing down the top of the bushy evergreen.

A few minutes later Nonie and I got things under control and had the yearlings together and moving toward the gate when we saw Bob's head pop up as he rode straight up and out of the wash. The white horse's nostrils were flared and so were Bob's. He hollered for me to get through the gate in front of the yearlings and go on to open the next gate leading to the corral and the large gathering pasture.

At a trot I hurried through the gate and followed a trail up a small hill and through greasewood and sagebrush on my way to the gate. Hustling to get off, get the gate open, then get back in the saddle before they arrived, I then positioned Nanner so we could turn the heifers through. Nervous and high-strung, Nanner spun around and bobbed his head, acting like he was getting ready to buck. Reaching down to the front of his right shoulder, I began vigorously rubbing with my glove while talking softly to him. Again he surprised me when his entire body relaxed and he stood perfectly still. We were buddies from that moment.

Straining my neck, I watched for the riders and their tiny herd to come over the hill, but they didn't. I waited some more, listening to the rain tap on my hat and slicker. Nobody showed up.

"Gee whiz, Nanner," I said. "What do you suppose is goin' on now?"

We trotted back the way I'd come. I spotted them coming over the hill just inside the gate. We worked together and, finally, we put the three red heifers through the second gate and on to the big field where they immediately started munching on belly-high grass.

As we rode across the bridge over Red Creek, we headed to the tack shed laughing. "Well, I've got to say it. You were right, Nonie," Bob said. "I was really liking this horse until we started trying to put those heifers through the gate. He went plumb goofy. When we came back off the top of that hill, I tried everything to get him stopped. I pulled his head clear around until his nose was touching my leg, but he just kept going like a bat out of heck. We were headed right for that big wash so I gave him his head so he could see, but he barely slowed down. He plowed straight off the bank, and up the wash we went."

"Well," Nonie said, "you know I hate to say I told you so, but I *told* you so. He scared me the minute I got on him."

Stepping off Nanner, I asked, "Well, what took you guys so long when I left to open the gate?"

"Oh, yeah," Nonie said. "That was simply amazing. I had the heifers right up to the gate. If I'd had just two more seconds, they would have been through. Then behind me I hear this thumping, thundering commotion and then *zingo*, there went Bob on that crazy white horse running right up through the middle of the yearlings, scaring them sideways. Up the fence line the yearlings went. The look on Bob's face was priceless—like he couldn't believe it was happening. So there I go again, trot-trot-trot after 'em. When

I looked back, Bob and that horse were really goin' the rounds. They were up in the air, running sideways, and jumpin' over sagebrush, cedars, and you name it."

Bob shook his head. He was always on the best horse in the bunch, or he made it seem that way because of the way he got them to perform. "I still can't believe it," he said. "And then, just as soon as we came through the gate with the yearlings, he calmed down and from then on acted like an old broke horse."

Pulling the saddle and blanket off Nanner's back, I grunted as I carried them into the building that had once served as a schoolhouse. "Yeah," I said as I laid the saddle over the log saddle rack. "We were quite the cowhands today. It's a darn good thing those girls were so gentle or they would have quit the world."

Laughing, Bob said, "Yep, they'd still be running."

"Yeah," Nonie said, "and we'd still be chasin' 'em, too."

When we turned the horses loose, they went to roll, and we undid our chaps and hung them from nails on the log beams of the shed. Still giggling at ourselves, we walked through the rain toward the house.

"I'll peel the potatoes and fry the steaks if you two will do the rest," Bob said as we wiped our feet and went inside.

A while later we were at the table eating grilled steak, crispy fried potatoes and onions, pickled beets, fresh corn on the cob, and sliced garden tomatoes and cucumbers. By the time we finished eating, Nonie and I were droopy. It seemed impossible we had made the trip from home just today.

The first few days breaking in were the roughest, but it was all tough, and there was no easy way around it. Spending endless hours in the saddle was brutal on the body. But riding together again—that was splendid for the spirit.

The white horse went back to Rock Springs. Nonie named the sorrel Sarley, and he soon became her trusted partner as Nanner was mine. But then, just after we rode out one morning, Nanner began to limp. Looking down, I saw blood oozing all along the hairline above both front hooves. It broke my heart to find out that his problems were severe and I would never ride him again.

❧

One day I was riding Brandy, a pretty sorrel quarter horse with a blaze face. Bob's son, Rick, who was in school in Rock Springs and would soon turn sixteen, had outgrown the old gelding. The horse was a well-seasoned cow horse and a dream to ride. Bob called his horses like Brandy the grandpa horses. They usually didn't have much work to do and were even pampered now and then. Brandy still had a lot of heart, seeming to have the desire to work, but he had arthritis in his knees. I took great care with him.

Nonie, Bob, and I had earlier split up, riding the Willow Creek Butte area. Brandy and I were climbing up the side of the Butte and had nearly made it to the top when suddenly he froze in position with his head up, ears forward, and eyes big. Then I saw it: a small herd of elk running straight at us. I sat still and Brandy never as much as twitched an ear.

About twenty head, including bulls, cows, and calves, surrounded us and stopped. Holding their heads high and throwing them from side to side, the elk whiffed the air, obviously baffled by our strong scent. Because we didn't move, the elk never saw us. For two or three minutes the elk milled around before moving away at a trot. I couldn't wait to tell Nonie when I saw her riding toward me.

"Did you see those elk?" I hollered. "I was sitting right in the middle of them."

"I sure did. I loped along with them for quite a ways and they never knew I was there."

Another time we watched an odd partnership between a badger and coyote traveling together, and then there was that cottontail we saw snuggled up and napping with a doe and her fawn. There was a constant flow of such wonders.

Days continued to pass and we brought in herd after herd of yearlings. Sometimes the herds of cattle were small, other times they were one or two hundred strong.

The rainy spell gave way to the sun and the days grew hot, so hot that we sometimes had to let the cattle, with slobber stringing from their mouths, stop a few minutes to rest. My black chaps felt limp as though they were melting when they absorbed the potent rays, causing the front of my thighs to sting. Meadows no longer wet had their topknots singed, and the grass turned yellow and crisp. But there was often a lingering scent of the water hidden just below the surface. The luscious smell teased the nostrils of animals and humans, making us long for a drink.

Sometimes cinnamon-like dust boiled into the air from hooves trotting off hills, filling our eyes and noses and crunching between our teeth. Pulling the silk scarf tied loosely around my neck over my nose and mouth helped block some of the dust but added to the reasons to sweat.

The shipping date was just about a week away and, except for some hard to find stragglers, most of the yearlings were all gathered into one large pasture called the big field. My husband, Mike, his sister Charlotte (whom he had just picked up at the airport in Rock Springs), and our nine-year-old son, Nick, arrived. Charlotte had flown from California with her suitcase, saddle, and a large batch of homemade chocolate chip cookies in tow. Mike would spend the weekend riding with Bob and then would come back next weekend to help us ship and then take Charlotte to the airport.

Blue-eyed and blonde, Charlotte was delightful, hard working, and witty, and she often soothed our weariness by giving us reasons to laugh. The day after arriving, she was with Nonie and me in the bottom of Tepee Creek. We were trailing a few head of contrary yearlings along the creek bed, and the cattle didn't want to go. They took off on every trail leading out of the creek, running up steep banks that averaged ten or twelve feet high. Nonie and I hurried up the trails, worked to outrun the yearlings, circled in front of them, and then turned them back down the trails and into the creek. As I chased a couple of yearlings along a shale bank, I saw Charlotte look up from the creek below and say, "You and Nonie are the bravest people I know." I laughed.

Charlotte was a good rider and owned horses in California. But she was not accustomed to this kind of riding, and she had never, during her recreational trail rides, encountered country like this: trails so sheer there was real danger of a horse coming over backwards. The trails cut deeply through banks in gouges so narrow our knees scraped as twisted arms of brush and their dangling roots clawed at us. She cringed at washed-out places where it seemed the very bones of the earth were exposed, leaving the trails frail and unstable. Riding up or down the steep terrain terrified her.

"You're doin' all right, Char," I answered. "You just stay behind that bunch and keep them headed down the creek. We need you there."

Wearing a giant fever blister on swollen lips by the end of the week, Charlotte was sun- and windburned, had stiff and aching hips and knees, was often blowing black dirt from her nose, and had legs bruised and rubbed raw—just like the rest of us. But from the beginning she had proved herself a natural when it came to ranch work.

Mike and Nick returned two nights before shipping and brought along Nonie's teenaged children, Brent and Ginger. Rick and his mother drove in right behind them. A few minutes later, Clyde and Velma Thompson arrived and we happily carried in the food Velma had prepared for supper. Soon we sat down to the treat of a huge pot of beans and ham, coleslaw, homemade buns, and fruit-filled vanilla cake.

The next day there was a flurry of tasks to do and we were so happy to have such good help. Some cooked and did household chores while others rode to find the last of the yearlings. The cattle were sorted and the replacement heifers Bob wanted to keep were cut from the herd. Last thing that evening, we all worked at doing corral alterations and filling a large water tank in the back of a pickup time after time with creek water, which we sprayed on the ground in the large set of corrals.

The gas motor on the spray pump was loud and obnoxious, often refusing to start unless it was babied. Once I made the mistake of barely touching it with my wrist. The burn was so deep, it took weeks to heal. The attached hose wasn't very long, but it made up for its short length with its girth. Regardless of who the person was walking behind the slow-moving truck in charge of manhandling the hose as it sprayed, the hose usually did things its own way. Jerking this way and that, it doused not only the ground but also anything or anyone in the vicinity. Cold creek water mixing with the coolness of the evening air wasn't pleasant.

In spite of the rigmarole, we would be thankful we had done this job come morning. Dampening the powdery ground to help hold down the dust dramatically improved working conditions when the corrals were filled with trampling hooves.

The next morning it was cold with just the slightest hint of daylight coloring the black above the mountains when we walked from the tack shed with our bridles. I held the metal bit in both hands, hoping to warm it some before asking my gelding to take it into his mouth. We were all nervous. This was it: the culmination of everything having to do with more than eight hundred head of yearlings. Timing and handling were crucial.

A few minutes later I shivered as we rode through the gate of the big field. None of us wore chaps or spurs because we would have to hit the ground running as soon as we got the yearlings in the corrals. Bob was an expert at handling yearlings and he taught us well, but getting the yearlings through both the pasture gate and then the corral gate without a wreck was far from certain because yearlings can be touchy and are prone to stampede. They could turn back on us before we got them corralled and run in all directions or even break through the fences and scatter. It was vital that the herd be handled quietly and with care. We all knew our positions and split up at the gate. From this moment we would not speak above a whisper.

Taking off at a trot on horseback, Nonie, Charlotte, and I headed down the fence line to the bottom of the huge field. Slowly we started the yearlings moving. The morning coolness made them feel frisky and ready to play. Suddenly one was crowded into the fence, causing the wire to squeak loudly. That started a reaction rippling forward. First seven, then nearly twenty, then a couple hundred began to lope. We stayed calm, giving them room, and the ripple was gone as quickly as it began. Breathing deeply, Nonie and I looked at each other.

Everyone's cattle came together, intermingling near a small reservoir. We saw Dad, the brand inspector, the cattle buyer, and the representative from Superior Livestock Auction who was a lifelong friend of ours, R.C. "Bob" Buckley. Each of the men was in his own pickup coming down the Hoy Dugway in front of the semi cattle trucks. Perfect. They would all be parked and ready at the corrals by the time we got there. Following the directions of Bob's hand signals, we began bending the river of cattle toward the corrals.

Several minutes later the leaders reached the gate opening and stopped, smelling the ground. "Come on, babies," Nonie whispered. "Go on through it."

The first went, then the second. Soon a flood of yearlings began moving into the corrals. Nonie and I laughed with relief as we hurried to get the tail end of the cattle through the gate before the others rushed back.

Charlotte had a wide grin when she said, "Hey, I told you guys there weren't going to be any problems. You did all that worrying for nothin'. I'm tellin' ya, good luck and good weather follow me everywhere!"

"Well, you just keep that up, Char, because we need you bad!" Nonie said.

"Yeah, that's for sure," I said. "But you better be careful. We might not let you leave!"

Quickly we jumped from our horses, threw the reins over corral poles, and ran to take our positions inside. A group of yearlings had already been weighed on the scales and were clamoring up the ramp, loading into one of the waiting trucks. Nonie went to help the men and Charlotte stayed with me. It was our job to empty one holding corral after another while filling the long, curved alley as soon as it was empty. Though we tried not to stress the cattle, it was inevitable that fresh manure would flip from hooves and tails, sometimes splattering us with green.

Things went smoothly and before long the women's work at the corrals was finished. Nonie, Char, and I rode our horses to the tack shed, got them turned loose, and then headed to the house to help Velma with breakfast.

The kitchen filled with people. Stacks of hotcakes, platters of eggs and sliced ham, and fresh cantaloupe and watermelon from Dad's garden in Vernal soon disappeared. When they finished up the paperwork, Bob and Dad were smiling at the gain the cattle had made.

Dad headed home to Vernal and Mike and Bob got ready to go to 4-J Basin to ride after cattle with rancher and friend John Raftopoulos.

As he walked out the door, Bob said, "You girls can just relax around here this afternoon while we're gone." But just a few seconds later, he stuck his head back in the door and grinned. "What you could do, though, if you want, is saddle up and take those replacement heifers over to Meadow Gulch. And while you're over that way, you might as well make a big circle and get a start on bringing in some cows and calves."

Nonie mumbled and squeezed out the dishrag. "Well, that was a pitiful afternoon off."

⁂

Time went by and Nonie, Bob, and I rode hard as yellow mountain slopes gave way to slick branches. The big field was gradually filling with black whiteface, red English, English cross, and Hereford/Angus range cows and their calves. The huge Limousin bulls were cut from the cattle herd and put into the bull pasture off the hill from the big field.

Riding behind a few head of cows and calves along the side of Pine Mountain one morning, I watched a cow walk across a small grassy spot that was damp with oozing spring water. Suddenly the innocent-looking ground swallowed her hooves and she began to struggle while sinking in the black mud to her shoulders. Luckily she quickly made her way safely out. Just then Nonie came over a small hill beside the bog and kicked Sarley into a fast trot to turn my cows.

"Don't go across that. It's a bog," I said. But she ignored me, making a beeline for the cows.

"Stop! That's a bad bog!"

It was too late. Sarley hit the mud and in an instant sank to his belly. I watched in horror as the gelding lunged and floundered, fighting fiercely. Nonie was jarred loose from the saddle and her feet yanked from the stirrups. Her legs flew straight into the air and she flipped upside down and into a nosedive. Bawling loudly, I screamed her name, certain her head would be crushed between Sarley's belly and the ground.

Seconds later Sarley jumped clear of the bog, and Nonie, covered with black mud, stood up laughing and said, "I'm okay. Everything's fine. That was fun!"

"You scared me so bad," I sobbed. "I just knew your head was gonna get squished."

Rubbing the back of her head, she giggled. "Nope, it didn't get squished, but it got a pretty good knot from that log lying there. You'll notice it's the only one anywhere around here and I had to hit it."

We rode on, trailing seven head of cows and calves along the side of the mountain. Sarley, the saddle, and Nonie each wore chunks and smudges of drying, stinky mud. As Nonie went ahead, I saw a long stemmed piece of yellow grass stuck on her back, which reached from the seat of her pants to the top of her neck. Its bearded top nodded with every step Sarley took. Filled with relief that Nonie wasn't hurt, it never once occurred to me to pull it off or even mention it.

After we spotted several more cows, we were soon in a battle. The cows threw their heads in the air and took off. Up and down the slope and around and through the trees we streaked. Hurrying to get in front of them, I shot around a cedar growing on a knoll and jumped my gelding across a narrow crevice. I pulled the horse to a stop, then I hollered and waved, sending the cows back toward the herd. It was then I took time to notice that the crevice did not simply run in a line; the deep crack was in a circle, surrounding my horse.

"Get offa there!" Nonie yelled from behind me. "That whole knob is about to break loose. Get off your horse and lead him back across. Now!"

I swung my leg over the gelding's rump and stepped down, knowing any second the ground could give way. After crossing the broken earth to solid ground, I quickly got back in the saddle and after the cows. The close call was already forgotten.

Finally we had seventeen head of cows and their calves walking single file along a good trail. Nonie left to climb higher to look for more cattle. All I had to do was keep the herd on the trail and we'd soon be off the point of the mountain.

As the trail tipped downward, the cattle began to trot. Though we were approaching an area heavy with timber, the trail bypassed it and we would barely graze its edge. But just then, far below but in our path, an elk hunter stepped into a clearing.

I'm not sure whether the hunter ever saw us, but the cows saw him. My gelding ran with everything he had through brush and over chunky rocks, but there was no stopping the determined mothers stampeding for the timber.

I left my horse when he could get no farther through the dense growth. Ducking limbs, I tore past scratchy pine bark and pushed through shrubs while trying to find a way to turn the cattle back. Heavy chaps and knee-high boots pulled on my legs, and each time the riding heels hit the ground my teeth jarred. My head throbbed against the band in my hat and my shirt grew sticky with sweat, even on the inside of my elbows.

When I stumbled against a fallen tree that was lodged about waist-high, my brain couldn't decide whether I should go over or under it. Pitching a heavy leg up and over the gray trunk, I lost my balance. The next thing I knew I was hugging that log with my arms and legs wrapped tightly around it. Twirling like a clumsy acrobat I held on, finally ending up dangling underneath, not more than a foot off the ground. I grunted as I got to my feet and caught one last glimpse of a cow's tail as the herd disintegrated, melting into the tangle of timber. I was defeated.

Later when I met up with Nonie and Bob, I was humiliated to admit that I'd lost my herd and feeling blue that a whole day's work had been for nothing. But when Bob rode up to Nonie and picked the long stem of grass off her back, we all laughed as Nonie and I told him the story of the bog. He said he'd heard my screaming clear on the top of Pine Mountain, but he'd figured we were just "cussin' cows."

Within a few days, a wet snowstorm gathered those seventeen head and brought them not only off Pine Mountain but also all the way to Meadow Gulch. I was glad about that, but the snow muddied the slopes and trails and sharpened the wind. By now the three of us and all the horses were losing weight and wearing down. The grass in the gathering field was not far from giving out.

Bob tapped his spurs against the sides of his gelding, leaned forward, and said, "Come on, Crow, you're almost done. You've got all winter to heal up."

We were relieved when we put the last of the cows and calves into the big field and closed the gate. There was still a lot of sorting to do.before shipping the calves, but we were lighthearted that our biggest job was finished.

Trotting toward the tack shed, we laughed at the squall peppering us in the face with sleet. We could laugh because we didn't know about the storms lining up on the battlefield. They had Red Creek in their sites, and they were coming.

Top: *Trailing yearlings off Cold Spring Mountain.*
Above: *Nonie after a long day of gathering cattle.*
Leftt: *Mike with Duchess and Hobo on Cold Spring Mountain.*

Top: *Bob, his son Rick, and Mike doing corral work at the Red Creek Ranch.*
Above: *Bob watering the corral to keep the dust down.*

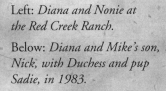

Left: *Diana and Nonie at the Red Creek Ranch.*

Below: *Diana and Mike's son, Nick, with Duchess and pup Sadie, in 1983.*

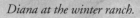
Diana at the winter ranch.

INTO THE STORM

Several days later, we woke to the sound of a light rain in the early morning darkness. It tapped against the window to make sure we knew it was back. The storms that were lined up kept coming at us, one after the other. The sound of rain used to bring me pleasure with its promise of life and honeyed air. Now it pinched at my spine.

The drizzling quickly grew into the fat drops of a downpour splattering the glass panes and rapping loudly on the roof. I knew there was no way the large cattle trucks could fight the gumbo mud, deep and slimy, to make it down the steep dugway leading to the ranch. They had been trying for the last three days. There had been a several-hour break in the weather the day before when the trucks could have crept in, but the cattle buyer's representative panicked and halted the trucks at the highway turnoff.

Bruised and worn out from the weeks of gathering cattle, I thought about Mike and Nick at home. *Why do I do this every year—come down here and half kill myself?*

Bob struck a match in the next room and a propane wall lamp yawned a soft glow. Beds creaked as everyone began to stir. Dad cleared his throat and Bob's teenaged son, Rick, moaned for more sleep. Both Rick and Dad had come for the weekend to help us ship the calves.

Nonie threw the covers back on her bed, and said, "I guess we might as well get up. I don't know what we're gonna do, but we've got to do something."

When I entered the kitchen, the windows were still coated black. The only sound was the dinging of a spoon in a mug of coffee. Dad sat with his forehead resting on his crossed hands on the tabletop. Mom would have taken one look at us and said we all looked like we'd been drawn through a knothole backwards.

Dad stood and walked to the window. Squinting to see into the dawn, he said, "It's snowin' now." He shook his head. "I've never seen the like. Things just won't gel. Everything we do lately goes sour."

Bob got to his feet. "What do you think, guys? I vote we head to the winter ranch with 'em. I can't stand to just sit here. We're running out of hay and the pastures are ate off. It's hard telling when this is gonna let up."

Nonie winced. "I don't know if we should do this, Bob. I mean I *really* don't know if we should do this."

"Yeah, but, Nonie, if we don't get them out of here now, when are we going to? It could keep this up for two solid weeks. We've got to get the cows over there anyway, and with the highway close, we can ship the calves from there."

It was settled. Bob and Dad both chained up their pickups and left to meet the cattle buyer at the highway near Maxon Ranch to make new arrangements. Before returning, they would leave one pickup at Uncle Billy Rife's deserted homestead that was halfway of the twenty-two miles to the winter ranch. The plan was we'd drive the cattle the eleven miles to Uncle Billy's, hold them there overnight, and get them to the winter ranch just after noon the next day.

Soon we were saddling up. I very reluctantly left my hat and spurs in the house, deciding instead to wear my boot overshoes and hooded yellow slicker. When we swung into our saddles, the cold leather chilled us from our centers both ways. The geldings smelled of wet hair, and mud oozed around their hooves at every step. They snorted into the cold, perhaps feeling the same dread as their riders. By the time we got to the big field, the storm had let up and it was just misting, giving us hope.

Before the herd was half gathered, it began to rain. I pulled the stiff hood of my slicker over my head and jerked off my gloves, hoping to keep them dry for at least a while. The number of cows and calves totaled nearly fifteen hundred head. None of them wanted to walk headlong into a storm, and they refused to leave the field. It took some time, but we finally shoved them through the gate and had the leaders starting the steep climb out of the basin. Pudgy flakes of snow began tumbling from the sky, quickly coating the sagebrush and cedars with dollops of white. Holding on to the sopped leather reins, my fingers turned rosy red.

Dad, Bob, and Rick went with the leaders and worked the sides of the herd. Nonie and I had the tail end. Nonie was on Sarley. He still tended to be a runaway. I was on Allisaun, a sorrel so tall that the first time I rode him he lunged into a long lope that snapped my head back and I nearly swallowed my tongue. Since then I had trusted him with my life many times.

Calves bunched up in the rear, confused and lost from their mothers. Convinced their mothers were somewhere behind us, about a dozen calves suddenly turned and streaked in several directions. Nonie and I whirled our horses around. The calves were on a dead run. She took off one way and I went another.

Running wide-open, Allisaun cleared muddied crevices and badger holes. Wet sagebrush grabbed at my feet and chaps as Allisaun's hooves and knees cracked through it. I was breathing hard and nearly choked when I sucked some feathery flakes of snow down my throat. Making it to the lead calf, I waved my free arm wildly and screamed, "Go back! Get back, you dirty little buggers. Turn!"

Our calves finally came together on the road, and Nonie and I fell in behind them on a trot. As we rubbed our horses on their necks, we were both exhilarated and laughing.

"I got them all turned but one," Nonie huffed. "He just wasn't going to turn for anything, and he was doing ninety-per when I got up beside him. He was eyeballin' me and I was eyeballin' him, and I'm thinkin', *He's gonna shoot off to the side any second, and I'm gonna have to stop this horse. Am I going to be able to stop this horse?* But when the calf turned, Sarley pulled right up. I'm so proud of this little horse."

"Yeah, but we haven't even got a good start yet," I said. "Good grief, I could throw a rock and hit the gate, we're still so close to the house. I hope this isn't a sign of what's ahead."

Just then we saw a wad of cattle coming off the hill, spreading into the cedars. I stayed with the calves and Nonie hurried Sarley to get in front of the mess. When Sarley kept sinking and sliding, I saw Nonie jump from his back and run a little ways. Each step got slower as mud built around her boots. Packing feet the size of snowshoes, she went out of sight into the cedars. I knew, though, no matter what it took, she wouldn't give up until the cows were turned.

When she caught up with me later, the cows were back on the road, and most of the mud had been scraped from her boots with a rake of sagebrush. Her face was flushed and her hazel eyes glassy.

"Criminy," she giggled. "With these heavy chaps and that mud gummed up on my boots, I'll bet my legs weighed a ton each. They got so rubbery I could hardly climb back on. Sarley and I are both worn out, and we still ain't even out of the dooryard."

The snow and rain took turns throughout the day. That same bunch of calves stayed in the rear and never passed up an opportunity to make a break for it. In most places the mud was ankle deep, tiring horses and cattle with every step. We hollered and whooped until our throats were raw. We shivered, longing for the sun to pick a hole through the dripping sky.

A bright spot in the day arrived about six hours into our trip when neighboring rancher Stan Jolly came along in his Jeep. Stan gave Bob the best he could offer our bedraggled crew when he handed him a package of sweet rolls and a cold pop apiece.

When Bob gave Nonie and me our pop, we hesitated. With her teeth chattering, Nonie said, "I don't think I want this."

"Oh, yes, drink it," Bob said. "I promise it'll warm you up."

With that positive notion in our heads, we took a couple of swallows. When the icy liquid hit bottom, Nonie looked at me and shuddered. "I think that pop just snuffed out what tiny bit of candle I had left."

Hour by hour the day wore on, and the cows never got more eager to face the storm. They had to be prodded constantly. I had long ago stopped feeling any resemblance to a spirited cowgirl. Nonie said I looked like a wilted yellow posy.

With the rubber-cushioned heels of my overshoes doing little more than pestering the gelding's thick hide, I said, "For cryin' out loud, Allisaun. I know you've about had it, but can't you take one single step on your own? Just a couple more miles and we can quit for the night."

I heard the jangle of spur rowels behind me. Turning in the saddle, I looked through the rain and saw three riders on fresh horses and decked out in dusters, big hats, and inlaid silver. As the Jolly girls and their Mexican hired hand loped easily through the brush, waving the skirts of their dusters and throwing loops with their lariats, the cattle hurried along the road like they hadn't done once all day.

I was thankful for our neighbors' help, but, feeling homelier by the moment, I wanted to wither out of sight. I tried to make my way up the side of the herd to put some distance between us, but Bob waved at me to go back. All I could do was pummel Allisaun's ribs and long for this day to be over.

Just before dark we climbed into the stretch-cab pickup and headed for home. We bucked greasy mud the entire way.

Barely a heartbeat later, it was dawn, and we carved our way back to Uncle Billy's. None of us had our voices; the day before we'd left them scattered along the trail.

Bob shifted in his seat behind the steering wheel and said hoarsely, "I guarantee that the worst is over. The storm's lifting and the cows'll be full and ready to trail. They'll string out going down Rife's Rim, and we'll hit the winter ranch by early afternoon."

We barely had our feet in the stirrups when it started to pour. Calves splintered in all directions, and the cows balked at leaving the willows. With our ropes down, popping the cattle on the hind ends, we fought them through the gate and started up the hillside leading to Rife's Rim.

We were a quarter of the way up the hill when I saw Nonie and Bob leaning toward each other in their saddles with their eyes bugged out and neck veins swelling. They were screaming at each other in frustrated squeaks. Nonie spun her horse around and trotted past me.

"I'd like to wring his neck," she croaked. "He thinks he's the only one who knows how to do anything. And I've lost my damn rope." Her raspy voice washed away with the rain as she trotted down the hill to pry cattle from the gully.

We topped the hill on Rife's Rim, but the cattle didn't string out. We each skirted the herd, back and forth, staying steadily on the move. Cold rain and a brisk breeze washed our faces relentlessly. My knees screamed, my toes went numb, and the dampness seeped through my slicker and coat and into my skin. I wanted to cry but only allowed myself an occasional whimper.

Nonie rode up. With her entire body shaking, she chattered, "Are wwwe having ffun yet?"

I broke into a coarse laughter. "Are you okay? Your boots must be soaked clear through."

"Yeah, they are," she said pitifully and rode on.

It was late by the time the winter rangeland came into view, and the shroud of clouds and rain was quickly growing darker. When we crossed Highway 430, a mere mile from the winter ranch gate, nightfall smeared around us like wet, black pulp. Unbelievably, with such a short distance to go, minutes swelled into hours as we inched the cattle forward.

We were beyond exhaustion. The blackness was so intense that at times I thought Allisaun was backing up instead of moving forward. His left hind leg began to jerk and I thought he was caught in wire. When I realized he wasn't caught but was having muscle spasms, I got off and led him.

Walking a ways off the road, I tapped the ground with my toes before each step to make sure I didn't fall in a hole. I thought I saw a cow beside me, and I moved toward it and yelled with what little voice I had and slapped the ground behind it with the bridle reins. When it didn't move, I walked up against it and discovered it was a bush. A few minutes later I thought I was walking beside a six- or seven-foot-high white embankment. I reached out my hand, I waved it back and forth, expecting to touch it. I was astounded when the illusion suddenly flopped on its side and flattened out. It was the road.

Following the sound of give-out voices, Nonie and Sarley swept the edges of the herd. Without warning the earth dropped from beneath them as a deep wash swallowed them whole. Miraculously Sarley stayed on his feet as he scrambled off the bank of the wash and scurried up the other side. Nonie squalled, "Whoa-ho, taco!"

and grabbed the top of her head. Sarley dropped his nose to the ground and from then on kept it there.

Keeping a constant, aching strain on my eyelids, I held them open as wide as possible. I couldn't believe it when I realized I was face to face with cattle turning back! Crying out, I hurried to get back in the saddle. After I got my foot in the stirrup, I reached up with my right hand and grabbed the back saddle strings. Tearing away from the saddle, the strings turned to mush in my hand. I scrambled up the side of the gangly gelding and made it to the saddle. Frantic that we were losing the herd, I did everything I knew to turn the cattle around.

Several minutes later I tingled with relief when I heard Nonie's voice. "Dad says we're at the fence. He said he found it when his horse bounced off it. They were against the fence, that's why the cattle turned back. I'm pretty sure we've got 'em stopped, but we've got to hold 'em 'cause the gate's locked and Bob's gone runnin' on foot to the house to get a key."

Finally, we heard a motor and saw headlights. Soon Bob had the gate unlocked and his old pickup Green positioned to shine its headlights onto the roadway and gate. As rain flickered across the light, cattle poured through the opening.

We were giggly as we rode toward the corral to unsaddle. This job was done!

It was a little after ten o'clock when we peeled off our saturated chaps and slickers in the warmth coming from the wood cookstove in the elderly log house. Severely dehydrated, we gulped coffee made in a blackened pot before heading back to Red Creek.

Packed into the cab of the battered but reliable four-wheel drive ranch truck, we etched our way easily through the mud as we topped the hill above Uncle Billy's and started down. Just when someone bragged on Bob's driving, Green took a fit and slid one way, then another, and dove off the left side of the road, landing in the deep borrow pit. With the truck cradled at a sharp angle, we all sat still and in a stupor as we stared straight ahead. The windshield wipers thumped in perfect rhythm, back and forth.

Squashed against his door, Bob finally broke the spell when he grunted, "Is-somebody-going-to-get-out?"

The other pickup wasn't far. Dad walked down the hill to get it while Bob got out a tow chain. A yank or two later and the truck was back on the road.

Nonie and I rode with Dad. We made it only to the bottom of the hill before we got stuck and Bob had to pull us out of the ditch. Later, the trip down the treacherous Hoy Dugway, mostly sideways, was terrifying. Nonie gained a blood blister on her finger from a death grip on the window handle.

It was one in the morning when we shuffled into the kitchen. Dad looked down and said, "Well, lookee here, I've walked out of one overshoe somewhere." No one was surprised.

After a bowl of soup we got ready for bed. Sliding between the covers, I could hardly bare to think about everything we'd been through. Closing my eyes, all I could see were cows.

Rain began patting the roof and sliding gently down the window. Because I was warm now, and the cows were safely at the winter ranch, the sound of the rain soothed me.

I knew why I was there. I knew why Bob lived this life and why Nonie and I joined him every chance we got. There is where we were most alive—riding through the brush on the back of a horse. It's from where we came. It's what we loved and who we were.

Bill at the Red Creek Ranch

Opposite, top: *Allisaun, waiting to start the day at the Red Creek Ranch.*
Opposite, bottom: *Diana and Allisaun at Meadow Gulch.*
Top: *Diana on Allisaun, driving cattle at the Red Creek Ranch.*
Bottom: *Yearlings at Cold Spring Mountain*

Bob riding Howdy.

AT THE DIMMING OF THE DAY

Golden autumns came and went as colored leaves fell upon amber ponds and drifted with our stories across shadowed roads and old cattle trails. In the fall of 1992, history whispered to us as together we rode the rimrock along the edge of our time.

We heard the crackling of grasshoppers in flight and smelled a minty-sweet mix of pine, meadowland, and sage as we scoured the summer range on Cold Spring Mountain. After a couple of weeks, we had gathered nearly seven hundred yearling steers.

There on the mountain, where sturdy logs of homestead cabins once stood true, crumpled walls now leaned into the seasons. Aspens grew up through their hearts, and chipmunks played tag in and out of hollow places. Grandma and Grandpa Taylor's cabin, aged but strong, still sat on a hill above a fast-flowing spring. But the cabin Dad built at the head of Galloway Draw when he was twenty-four and the Parsons cabin in Brown's Park Mom worked so hard to save had both been burned to the ground by persons unknown.

In a soft and weathered voice, Dad said to me, "It's not but just a little while until the things you've planned and the things you've built are gone. It's family that really counts, and family that lasts. Your mother was awful proud of her big family—and I was awful proud of her."

But the family had not held together in the way we had all taken for granted and expected. Without Mom's steady and calming strength at the center, the three older and three younger of us came apart. The bond that was once proud and held strong by the laughter, loyalty, and love we had all known so well in our youth was now ill-treated and pitiful. It was with great sadness that I watched personalities, choices, and life-paths break Mom and Dad's family beyond repair. I could feel Mom's tears on my heart, but I also sensed that she had an understanding of it all that reached far beyond my comprehension. And, thankfully, no matter what, Nonie, Bob, and I continued to hang on to each other for dear life.

⚘

It was at first light when Bob, Nonie, Charlotte, Mike, and I rounded up the steers in the mountain holding pasture and headed them through the gate. Rays from the rising sun mingled with dust to form a coppery haze as cattle and horsebackers strung out along the edge of the timber on grassy, sage-covered hills. Mike and Bob rode point, Nonie and I rode the sides, and Charlotte brought up the rear. Slapping ropes against our chaps, whistling, and sometimes hollering, we moved the herd toward Red Creek.

This year I'd been riding both a chestnut called Warrior and the beautiful gelding that had been Bob's favorite at outrunning the wild horses of Douglas Mountain, Hobo. But Warrior had developed a sore back and Hobo was tired and needed the day off, so I chose to ride Handsome, the only fresh horse left. The sorrel's usual job was being a kid's horse.

Acting perky and polite, Handsome started the day off just right. But within a couple hours, when Handsome decided it was quitting time, he reminded me of a buckskin I once knew named Comet. I worked myself into a lather trying to convince the stubborn sorrel that we had at least five more hours to go. While yearlings moseyed off enjoying a morning snack, the only action I got out of Handsome was a few steps of a stiff trot punctuated by jarring crow-hops, which were really beginning to tenderize my tailbone.

Suddenly from another realm, Bob galloped toward me with-the-greatest-of-ease on his powerful gelding, Howdy. Following him and doing the work of two cowboys was his dog, Smokey.

Looking down his nose, Bob passed by while announcing, "You'd better make that horse *move*."

Bleary-eyed, panting, and ready to challenge both him and Handsome to a fistfight, I yelled at his dust, "You otta try it, you...you snot!"

When I finally won the battle with Handsome, I rode up to Charlotte. In a parched voice, I included several choice descriptions of my brother when I told her my troubles.

"Geez," she said. "He's always nice to me. When I told him a while ago I had no feeling left in my body from my hips down, he told me to just go ahead and chase after the cattle on foot till I felt better." We almost got the giggles but couldn't make the effort to laugh that hard.

Just then Bob rode up. With a sheepish grin, he said, "Hi, guys. Greek's got the leaders, so I thought I'd come ride with you for a minute." Then suddenly serious, he crossed his wrists on the saddle horn and said, "I don't know of any other five riders in the country that could bring this many yearlings off the mountain in this good of shape."

It was the usual way of things. From the time we were kids, one minute Nonie and I had visions of getting Bob down on the ground in a choke hold, and the next minute we'd find ourselves tending melted hearts.

⁂

Bob had his own way of watching over us. When we rode after cattle, spreading out and covering great distances in a day, Bob almost always knew precisely where we were. He usually appeared from nowhere when we were in a serious jam and needed him most.

Once Bob thundered between Nonie and a huge black bull she was trying to turn, startling both her and the bull. His face was pale and his lips white around the edges when he told her in a stern voice over his shoulder, "That bull was gonna take you!" With his rope down, he stayed on the heels of the bull, taking him away at a lope. Nonie had seen no sign of the danger.

Although I was pushing seven head of yearlings in unfamiliar country one day, I was positive I knew the way home. Riding Mike's smooth-gaited chestnut mare, Duchess, I had the yearlings trailing along fine up a creek that had high, steep banks on both sides. I just needed to watch for a certain area where a fire had scorched the earth and burned a couple of cedars. That would be my signal to drive the cattle out of the creek. There I would hit a good trail that would take us to the house. But the farther we went, the more the surroundings didn't seem right, and I started to feel uneasy. When nightfall began stalking us, my eyes searched in vain for the landmark. Following the cattle through a skinny canyon-like passage, I watched large hunks of earth dangle above as though a slight breeze could break them loose and send them crashing down.

Just as we came out of the canyon, two yearlings took off up a bank, stopping in a patch of willows toward the top. As Duchess lunged up the sandy bank to get above them, I was in tears and giving the wayward cattle a loud bawling out. Topping the hill, I stopped suddenly and blinked. There, carved into the near dark no more than ten feet away, sat Bob on his horse with a smile on his face.

"Oh, my bro!" I cried.

I soon felt absolutely foolish when I learned I was in a different creek from the one I thought. But I was so happy, I didn't care that I was never going to live it down. And about the gaunt passage, Bob said, "You came through *the narrows*." Shaking his head, he laughed, "That's one place I won't ride."

Another time, Nonie was alone on the side of a mountain peak fighting a bunch of cattle that refused to trail. She worked while riding her horse and running on foot, but the harder she tried, the worse the cattle were about dribbling off the trail and either taking off or hiding in the cedars.

Hot and worn out, Nonie screamed, "Where in the *heck* is everybody?!"

"Right here," Bob answered in the distance.

Surprised, Nonie raised her eyes and saw him waving to her from a high peak two draws over. Instantly uplifted, she felt her strength return as she watched him make his way to help her.

Other times, though, he convinced us to do the darnedest things. Whatever the job might be, it always seemed natural to do it, simply because he said so. Such was the time Bob stopped his pickup on the road near Meadow Gulch when he saw a sickly, whiteface cow standing alone in the sagebrush. Sending Nonie to get the cow, he went to open the gate to the pasture.

Walking through the brush, Nonie was looking down and not paying attention as she drew closer to the animal. When she looked up, she was startled to see the cow bobbing her head, obviously on the fight. When the cow charged, Nonie ran backward with her arms outstretched, using the palms of her hands as a shield. The same instant the cow bumped her hands, Nonie tripped and fell down. Trotting past with her nose in the air, the cow then ran up the side of a hill where she stopped and switched ends. Never once looking Bob's direction, the cow didn't take her eyes off Nonie as she made her way back to the pickup.

"Okay, now. That cow hates you," Bob said. "So go stand in the gate and holler at her. She's gonna take to you again. Wait till just before she hits you, then step aside and she'll go through the gate."

"I'm not getting paid for this, ya know," Nonie said.

"Oh, yeah, you are," Bob nodded. "You're gettin' a nickel a day and all the water you can drink."

A few seconds later, Nonie found herself standing in the gate waving her arms and yelling at the cow. The cow took aim and headed for her at a run. When the cow was only a few steps away, Nonie jumped behind a brace post and the cow barely brushed her sleeve as she sailed through the gate. Hurrying to join some other cattle feeding in the meadow, the cow never looked back.

"You make pretty good bait!" Bob laughed. And so it went. . . .

⁂

By mid-afternoon, Bob, Nonie, Mike, Charlotte, and I arrived at Red Creek with the herd of yearlings. They were shipped on schedule. Then we started riding to bring in the cows, calves, and bulls. Just before Charlotte left for home, she amazed herself and tickled us when she faced her deep fear of riding on steep, rugged terrain and demonstrated that grit comes along naturally when doing this work. Volunteering, she rode alone up the side of a mountain, stayed high checking for cattle, then later rode down a steep trail to the floor of the basin.

"I don't do ledges yet," she sparkled. "But this year, I do mountains!"

Almost a week later, Nonie, Bob, a hired Navajo named Herb, and I had already put in nearly a full day's riding when Bob decided to take Nonie, me, and our horses, Hobo and a blue roan named Blue, in the truck and trailer and drop us off on Tepee Mountain where Bob had earlier seen about twenty head of cows and calves.

It was hunting season, and our thin and satiny fluorescent-orange vests flapped wildly as our horses trotted into the wind whipping across the face of the mountain. Gathering the cattle from ridges and draws, Nonie and I got them all together in a bunch and started them down. Behind us we noticed a pickup pull to a stop high on a rocky point. We both winced when we turned to see two rifles pointed straight at us.

Knowing we were being watched through rifle scopes, we rode into a small but thick grove of aspens that clung to the angular terrain. But in this shaded place there was mud, and it was half-frozen. Blue and Hobo slipped, caught their footing, then nearly fell again. We got off but couldn't stand up and both landed on our rumps.

"Well, what do you think, Nonie?" I asked.

Carefully getting to her feet, Nonie answered, "I say let's get back on these horses and trust them to get us the heck out of here."

They slipped, slid, and did some scrambling, but the geldings made it to dry ground. Moments later we hollered at the cows and took off down the mountain behind them. In a playful mood, the cattle ran through the sagebrush and across a sloping meadow. We couldn't help laughing. The cows bucked with their tails kinked, and the roly-poly calves looked like bouncing balls with tails stuck straight in the air.

Before long we slowed the pace, having left the mysterious rifles far behind. Though the hunters were probably just curious, the hair on the back of our necks took a while to settle.

As we moved through cedars and creamy-red gullies at a walk, we felt the air grow still and cool as the sun went down. Soon a tiny hint of late evening blue was all we had to light our way. But before long a glow began on the skyline of the hill in front of us. Crossing a little creek at the bottom of the hill, we started to climb. We knew the area was covered with deep holes and eroded fractures.

"I wish that moon would hurry up," I said.

By the time we got up the hill, my wish came true. But the brilliance of the enormous moon was so dazzling that splinters of it stabbed us in the eyes. Getting off our horses, we waded into the black sea before us and, at times, felt our way through the maze on hands and knees while trying to keep the cattle together and going the right way.

A couple hours later we passed near the house, taking our herd of cattle to the big field. Delicious smells of supper stirred round in the air as we were greeted by happy voices. Mike, Nick, and Nonie's two kids, Brent and Ginger, had arrived for the weekend.

When Nonie and I walked through the door, Bob was standing at the stove tending to sizzling skillets. Grinning he said, "Everybody was sure getting worried about you two. But I told them there was no question that you'd get here, and when you did, you'd have all the cattle."

Compliments from Bob were hard to earn. This one tumbled into the center of our spirits and lodged there with another he'd given us not long ago. On the day we shipped the yearlings, Dad told us he overheard Bob at the corrals talking to a friend, Floyd Workman. Bob said, "If you want to see how to put yearlings in the corral, you just watch those girls."

After all the cows and calves were gathered, we worked for several days under Bob's direction, meticulously sorting and preparing to ship the calves. By now Bob had achieved great success and had gained an impressive reputation in the arena of the cattle buyers. The herd of cows and bulls he'd handpicked combined with award-winning land management and grazing practices resulted in highly valued calves. We were proud that, for several years, the prices paid for Bob's calves topped the sale at a livestock video auction broadcast nationwide on satellite television. His blue eyes filled with tears one day when he said, "I sure wish Mom could have seen this."

As usual none of us slept very well the night before shipping, afraid something had been left undone or the alarm wouldn't go off. But dawn came at last, and by its light we rode through the gate of the big field.

Tubby calves hurried to suck and the warm milk made bubbles around their mouths. Some stretched, others butted heads in play, while some other calves enjoyed getting their hair combed by their mothers' wide tongues. None of them seemed worried as they walked beside their mothers. But from the moment the cattle surged as a mass into the corrals, the gentleness of their morning erupted into bellowing bedlam. We had to ignore the deafening bawls of the cattle and our feelings of sorrow for them as we worked at the fast-paced process.

Exhaust from semi cattle trucks curdled the air as the trucks grunted into position. The alley was filled and refilled as the mothers were peeled away from the calves and put in holding corrals. The calves were brand-inspected, pushed onto scales to be weighed, then headed up ramps. Little hooves clattered and the metal ramps jangled as the flow of the work went on. At last the loaded trucks slowly climbed the Hoy Dugway and disappeared, taking the calves on their far-away journey.

When Bob and Mike returned to Red Creek that afternoon after helping neighbors at the Maxon and the Jim Ramsay ranches ship their calves, the corral gates creaked as we opened them wide. Standing back, we watched the rush of mothers frantic to search the fields. A thin, solid black cow that had been crippled over the summer tried to hurry. Her hind hooves glanced off each other, making clicking noises as she went. She'd raised a beautiful calf. Bob spoke gently to her, then he told us how he admired them, these range cows.

They had given life to their calves on the open range where often predators paced nearby. Maybe the calving place was in a sheltered ravine or tucked away in the cedars or beneath the shade of mouse-ear buds on cottonwood trees. Together through the summer they nuzzled, tugged on grass, and chewed their cuds. Now the mothers looked and called, finding no trace in the corners of the wire-hemmed pastures. Through the evening and then the night, their bawling continued, and the sound saturated the lemon light of the moon.

The next day, and two more after that, their voices dried and cracked. White faces became marbled with broken saliva webs and streaks of dusted tears. One by one the mother cows surrendered. In the end there was silence.

The cows needed this time to strengthen. Their hooves were already crushing ice tatting along the edges of the creeks. Soon they would lift their heads and smell wintertime on the sighs of a silver breeze. Then, outlasting blizzards, relentless wind, and nights of awesome cold, they would search for food and wait for spring to sprinkle green and warm the places beneath the cottonwoods, within the cedars, and in the sandy-soft ravines.

⚭

Tasks surrounding this year's gathering and shipping were quickly winding down as Nonie, Bob, and I drove a herd of bulls late one evening along an old road through the big brush pasture so we could put them through the bottom gate. From there they would be free to join the other bulls and make their way down Red Creek to Richard's Gap to spend the winter. Because the bulls were cranky and inclined to fight, we split them up. Nonie and Bob trailed nine head in front, and I followed a ways behind with five.

That morning I couldn't believe it when Bob said to me, "I'm giving you Hobo. I know you love him. When you go home this time, I think you should take him. He belongs to you now." Patting the handsome gelding on the neck, I noticed how soft the air felt tonight for late October.

An offering of perfection painted the surrounding dusk. Sunset was in full bloom and we trailed the bulls straight toward its grand swirls and streaks of peach, rose, and gold. The deep *mmmmmm-muh, mmmmmmmuh* sound from the bulls floated into the layers of dust hanging above the sagebrush. Ancient aromas of open country mingled so strongly that I could taste them on my lips. Smiling, I watched the harmony of Nonie and Bob in silhouette against the glowing sky.

It was as I was tucking it all into my memory that a dense sorrow fell so heavily upon me that I was forced to squeeze my eyes closed and take a deep breath. I didn't know what it meant. I couldn't know that we would never again ride the days of fall together. Or that as Bob's spring calves bucked on wobbly legs to the songs of meadowlarks, the extreme voltage alive within wires that powered a large irrigation pump would silently lie-in-wait for him to reach his hand out to it. I couldn't know that as killdeer sang and ran along moist banks, word of his death would come, shattering so many hearts and ending the ranching legacy that he had worked so hard to uphold. And that, soon after, Nonie and I would watch from some place outside ourselves as Dad's shoulders slumped and we sat quietly beside him while the Red Creek Ranch was sold and Allen Livestock dissolved. I couldn't know any of it. Instead, I pushed away the strange sadness and drank deeply from the last minutes of twilight.

"Well, this job's done, girls," Bob said as he closed the gate. "Let's head for the house."

The horses began to prance as we crossed the bridge over Red Creek. Riding side by side in the star dusk, we gave them more rein, and the geldings loped to the top of the hill overlooking the creek. The sound of our laughter and the clattering of hooves left us there and went together across the night, traveling beyond the white velvet of the coming snows and into the echoes of the past.

⚘

Red Creek flows on, passing through the silence of cedar and sage before joining the Green River to kiss the banks of the place once called the Brown's Park Livestock Ranch. As fallen embers of moonlight shimmer on the riffles and cottonwoods and willows brush their songs on the wind, we are there within the memories of a faded era with all the others who rode through timber and over ledges roping dreams. There, along the old Outlaw Trail, we searched for and found the best of ourselves.

Bob and Howdy in front of the tack shed at the Red Creek Ranch.

Top: *Bob on Howdy, counting yearlings through the gate*
Above: *Nonie and Bob, heading out to gather cattle.*

Opposite top: *Nonie, driving cattle on Cold Spring Mountain.*
Opposite left: *Diana, riding Hobo.*
Opposite right: *Nonie, graining horses at the Red Creek Ranch.*

ACKNOWLEDGMENTS

This book was created from a combination of my life-memories, recollections of stories I heard many times growing up, information gleaned from a wealth of interviews and informal visits with family and friends, and also books, letters, and other related material. There are many people to thank.

First and foremost, Mike Kouris, my dear husband, has my forever gratitude for his remarkable support, belief, and indispensable help bringing this book to life. Also, this book could not exist without Nonie and Bob Allen, my dearly loved sister and brother, who led me into a lifetime of adventure. Thank you, Nonie, for the many hours we spent together going over detail after detail while making sure our stories are accurate. I thank my son, Nick Kouris, who knows my heart so well, for the journeys of the heart he's taken with me to seek life's beauty in sight, sound, and word. My deep appreciation goes also to author and close friend Betty Starks Case, who, gently but with conviction, worked to persuade me that I had a authentic and wonderful story to tell. To my Uncle Jesse Taylor, who was a tremendous and priceless resource, I am so grateful. I'm also very grateful to my Uncle Wilson Garrison, who shared with me the heartbreaking details of his and Aunt Bessie's story. To John and Jo Story, Allen and Francis Taylor, and Clyde and Velma Thompson, I want to say how grateful I am for your love and encouragement. To all those who told their amazing stories to me, I humbly give my thanks.

I am deeply thankful to my grandfather and grandmother, C.M. and Nina Taylor, for following their dream to build a cattle ranch within the mountains. And to my beloved father and mother, Bill and Marie Allen, who gave me a beautiful upbringing, I owe everything.

Lastly, I wish to express my admiration for my wonderful publisher, High Plains Press. Thank you, Nancy Curtis, for your insightful belief in the manuscript from the beginning. Thank you also for the outstanding work you do. To the editor, Judy Plazyk, bless you for your amazing curiosity, perception, and skill.

SOURCES

I am indebted to the following individuals and sources who made this book possible:

Personal Interviews Taped by Author

Allen, Bob, March 1982; August 1987; October 1987.

Allen, Nonie, August 5, 1987.

Allen, William "Bill," June 6, July 13, July 15, October 10, 1981; October 1982.

Crouse, Stanley, Jr., May 15, 1983.

Garrison, E. W. "Wilson," July 14, 1981; October 10, 1981.

Kouris, Mike, August 1987.

Taylor, Allen, December 14, 1986; March 18, 2000; May 2001.

Taylor, Francis, October 22, 1982; May 2001.

Taylor, Jesse, May 26 and 27, October 10, October 11, 1981; March 1982.

Thompson, Clyde, July 4, 1987.

Letters to Author

Garrison, E.W. July 3, 1981; August 31, 1981; August 28, 1985.

Taylor, Jesse. August 3, 1981; September 21, 1981; May 10, 1982.

Books

Burroughs, John Rolfe. *Where the Old West Stayed Young*. New York: William Morrow, 1962.

King, Robert. "Colorado River Fishes Recovery Program." In *Species on the Edge, Quality Management Is Quality Growth, 2001 Endangered Species Management Report*. Utah Department of Natural Resources, Division of Wildlife Resources, 2001.

Tennent, William L. *John Jarvie of Brown's Park*. Utah State Office Bureau of Land Management, 1981.

Warner, Matt and King, Murray E. *The Last of the Bandit Riders*. New York: Bonanza Books, 1940.

Newspaper Articles

Brooks, Don, "Span Over Green Aids Utahns," *Salt Lake Tribune*, January 7, 1957.

Web Site Sources

Flaming Gorge National Recreation Area (n.d.). Retrieved November 26, 2006, from the Wikipedia Web site: http://en.wikipedia.org/wiki/Flaming_Gorge_National_Recreation_Area

U.S. Department of the Interior, Bureau of Reclamation. (n.d.) *Dams, Projects & Powerplants: Flaming George Dam*. Retrieved November 26, 2006, from http://www.usbr.gov/ dataweb/ dams/ut10121.htm

Utah Travel Center.com (n.d.). *Utah National Recreation Areas: Flaming Gorge*. Retrieved November 26, 2006, from http:// www.utahtravelcenter.com/nra/flaminggorge.htm

Other Sources

Allen, Marie. Her collection of correspondence, handwritten notes, newspaper articles, diaries, journals, interviews with Jesse Taylor and Minnie Crouse Rassmussen, and research and written histories of Lodore Hall and the Dr. Parsons Cabin. Also Marie Allen's accounts to the author about Marie's childhood in Brown's Park, life events, and stories told to Marie by her father, C.M. Taylor.

Besso, Georgann Radosevich. Her description of C.M. Taylor, including how much she admired him. Also her vivid first-hand account of the day Billie Dee Allen died.

Crouse, Stanley, Sr. Shortly before his death, Stanley visited our home in Rock Springs, Wyoming, and asked my dad to take him to the Brown's Park Livestock Ranch where Stanley grew up and later ranched. Dad did so, and at our ranch kitchen table, Stanley talked openly, telling the good and bad, about his dad, Charlie Crouse.

Folks, Merlene. Information about her great-grandfather, James "Jim" Marshall.

Strid, Nancy. Her letter written to Nonie Allen dated November 18, 2000.

Taylor, Murty. Stories about his life told by him to the author.

United States Department of the Interior, Draft Wild and Scenic River Study and Draft Environmental Statement, 1979.

INDEX

215–222, 227–236, *238, 239*
Allen Livestock, 35, *50, 52,* 157,
    174–175, 181, 236
Arbogast, Dr., 75

Bake Oven Flat, 83, 157–158,
    160, 180–181, 183
Baker, Bill, 117
Barger, Betty, 164
Bassett, Ann (*See* Bernard, Ann
    Bassett)
Bassett Ranch, 97–98
Beaver Creek, 89
Bennett, John, 97–98
Bentensen, Lula Parker, 182
Bernard, Ann Bassett, 66–67,
    97–98
Birch Creek, 131–133
Blevins, Freddie, 98
Blevins, Tom, 98
Blevins Ranch, 98
Braggs, Bill, 66
Bridgeport, UT, 67–69, 87, 89,
    92, 112–113, 157
Brown's Hole (*See* Brown's Park)
Brown's Hole Home Demonstra-
    tion Club, 99
Brown's Park, 15, 23, 31, 34, 36,
    38, 47, 65–77, 83, 87, *92,*
    96–104, 111–113, 117–118,
    126, 151–153, 157, 159–160,
    163, 174–175, 181, 183, 187,
    227
Brown's Park Livestock Ranch,
    15, 48, 67, 70, 76, *82,* 86,
    135, 157, 159–160, 163, 181,
    183, 236
Brown's Park Waterfowl Manage-

ment Headquarters, 154
Buckley, Kenneth, 96
Buckley, Martha, 96
Buckley, R.C. "Bob," 205
Buffham, Floy, 96
Buffham, Reg, 96
Bull Canyon, 97
Bureau of Land Management,
    159–160
Buxton, Nancy, 145, 154–156,
    188–189

Calder, Harold, 76
Carr, Harry, 118, 166
Carr, Sam, 112
Cassidy, Butch, 16, 26–27, 67,
    70–71, 98, 158, 181–182
Christensen, Grandma, 41–42
Christensen, Grandpa, 41–42,
    129
Christiansen, Willard E. (*See*
    Warner, Matt)
Clark, Patricia, 146
Clingan, Jerry, 143–144
Cold Spring Mountain, 33, 35,
    67, 74, 83, 99, *123,* 163, *211,*
    225, 227
Colorado, 15, 23, 33–34, 65–66,
    70, 71, 72, 83, 95, 97, 101,
    109, 113, 117, 151, 152, 154
Colorado River, 151–152
Compton, Marty, 143, 158
Crouse, Charlie, 26–27, *29,* 54,
    67–69, 89, 112, 126, 153,
    158, 182
Crouse, Mary, *29,* 67–68, 69
Crouse, Minnie (*See* Rasmussen,
    Minnie Crouse)

Diana Allen Kouris was raised on the historic Brown's Park Livestock Ranch in the "three corners" country of Utah, Colorado, and Wyoming. Surrounded with beautiful mountains and a lingering essence of the Old West, Diana thrived in the embrace of her family and their cattle ranching heritage.

Diana is also the author of the nonfiction book *The Romantic and Notorious History of Brown's Park*, which is a regional bestseller. Her work also appears in periodicals and an anthology. She lives with her husband, Mike, in the central part of Wyoming near Kinnear.

❧ NOTES ON THE PRODUCTION OF THE BOOK ❧

This book was simultaneously released in two editions.

A *limited edition* of only 200 copies was Smyth sewn,
bound in Sapphire Skies cloth,
embossed with silver Maximillias foil,
and wrapped in a full-color dustjacket with a non-scuff matte finish.
Each copy is hand-numbered and signed by the author.

The *softcover trade edition* is covered with ten-point stock,
printed in four colors, and coated with a special matte finish.

The text of both editions is from the Garamond Family by Adobe.
Display type is Algerian Mesa by ITC and Cyan by Wilton
with supplemental ornaments from Adobe Poetica
and Border Dingbats 1 by SMC.

The book is printed on fifty-five pound Nature's Natural,
an acid-free, recycled paper
by Thomson-Shore.

High Plains Press is committed to preserving ancient forests
and natural resources. We elected to print this title on 30%
postconsumer recycled paper, processed chlorine-free. As a
result, for this printing, we have saved:

13 Trees (40' tall and 6-8" diameter)
4,561 Gallons of Wastewater
9 million BTUs of Total Energy
586 Pounds of Solid Waste
1,099 Pounds of Greenhouse Gases

High Plains Press made this paper choice because our printer,
Thomson-Shore, Inc., is a member of Green Press Initiative,
a nonprofit program dedicated to supporting authors, publish-
ers, and suppliers in their efforts to reduce their use of fiber
obtained from endangered forests.

For more information, visit www.greenpressinitiative.org

Environmental impact estimates were made using the Environmental Defense
Paper Calculator. For more information visit: www.edf.org/papercalculator